LIFE
CODE
Second Edition
The Vedic Science of Life

BY
SWAMI RAM CHARRAN

Order this book online at www.trafford.com
or email orders@trafford.com

Most Trafford titles are also available at major online book retailers.

Printed in Victoria, BC, Canada.

ISBN: 978-1-4269-2625-9 (sc)

*Our mission is to efficiently provide the world's finest, most comprehensive book publishing
service, enabling every author to experience success. To find out how to publish your book, your
way, and have it available worldwide, visit us online at www.trafford.com*

Trafford rev. 1/13/2010

www.trafford.com

North America & international
toll-free: 1 888 232 4444 (USA & Canada)
phone: 250 383 6864 ♦ fax: 812 355 4082

ABOUT THE BOOK

THERE IS CONSCIOUSNESS IN EVERYTHING AROUND US.....

The universe is alive...it's a living, breathing, throbbing and heart-beating universe. Each of us is part and parcel of that universe, which makes us all combined and connected into one giant force we sometimes call God....or some cases the almighty forces of creation and destruction. I am so happy to have found this out at a very young age in my life. At the youthful age of 30, I did not realize that in my quest for the questions about life's existence, I would have found that the answers would really come to me with such an embrace so powerful that it almost squeezed the breath out of me. I had finally found the answers to life's most important questions like: Who am I? Where do I come from? Why am I here? And what is my purpose? I can now know when something will happen, how long it last, and when will it end. With such intellectual ecstasy, I am enjoying everyday in my life now. Not only that, what is more interesting is the fact that this great knowledge does not have any superstitious connections or any occult or mysterious connotations in any way. It is purely mathematical! It uses simple Arithmetic and Algebra in the basic forms! No complicated calculations! No advanced training is needed in math...all you need to know is addition and subtraction and the complicated problems of life can be solved and understood.

Dedicated

To my son Lucas and my Son-in-law Ernesto,
Both whom have mastered the science of Vedic Mathematics
While helping me to write this book

CONTENTS

CONSCIOUSNESS

"Why do people need this knowledge of the universe, Guruji?" asked the disciple, "and how will this knowledge help a person decide what kind of path to follow?"

"If you are traveling down the road or pathway and there are no exits or signs you could end up going on and on without having any idea where you are going. However if you are traveling on a road where the proper signs are posted you will know exactly where you are going and you will reach your destination. So also in life if you do not know where you are and where to stop or exit on the path of life, you will get lost, right?" the Divine Teacher inquired.

"How do the signs on the road help the traveler on the road find his destination and know where to exit or not?"

"Consciousness my dear boy!" the Teacher replied. "In this case the consciousness of another person (the sign maker or Guide) has helped to raise the consciousness of the traveler to a higher level by placing signs along the way so that he can have the knowledge of where to exit or not. As you can see, the prospective of the traveler on a path will change when another person with a higher knowledge has intervened. He is known as the Guru or Guide."

"Can the road we travel on be compared to our road of life from birth to death?" the student asked.

"Absolutely. All your choices and experiences in your life are the entrances and exits on the (road) path of your life," the Teacher responded.

The student thought deeply for a moment, and then asked, "Can you be the teacher of my life path, Oh Guru?"

PREFACE

"Life has an equation?" asked the Disciple.

"Yes, my dear child" answered the Guru calmly.

"Are you saying that I can actually calculate life, like I do in a mathematical equation?" asked the devoted student of the Guru once again, his eyes focused fully at the Divine Teacher.

"Precisely, my dear devote," said the Guru continuing, "There is a balance in the Universe and when the equilibrium or scale of balance is disturbed then an equation is formed to correct the balance, similar to your math equation in Algebra. Where a balanced condition writes as $A + B = 0$, which places both sides in a balance scale."

"Is that the same as karma?" asked the curious devotee.

"Yes. You can say that. Karma is simply 'Action = Reaction' which is the quality of all mathematical equations and still represents the fact that all things must exist in a scale of equilibrium in the universe."

"When this scale of equilibrium is disturbed, then the universe reacts in a negative or positive way, right?" the disciple inquired.

" Correct, then it results in an unbalanced equation of life above or below zero or created reality?" said the Guru as he continues, "Everything is in the balanced scale and the zero now become a 1, or 2 etc., for example if $A + B = C$ and B changes so will C."

"So you are saying that if I know the action I can predict the reaction side of the equation right Guruji?" replied the Disciple. "Isn't that exactly what Sir Isaac Newton did, when he came up with the Law of Motions?"

"Correct…" answered the Guru.

"Yes, but how can we apply the Equation principle to karma and our life?" asked the disciple.

"Well, let us say that everything has a beginning and end, do you agree?" asked the Guru.

"Yes, I do."

"Well if you add birth plus death you will get a balanced state of zero, wouldn't you? If you take the beginning of a string and add it to the end of a string does not the circle become a zero?" the Guru asked.

"Yes, and I suppose if the circle is cut at any point then we have a value of 1 again where one end becomes A and the other B. Now we have a beginning and an ending and many divisions in between."

"Absolutely correct my dear student. Now you have Equations of life happening between the Starting point and the ending point of the string which was once a Zero."

INTRODUCTION

"Guru-ji, what do I have to do to earn the saffron robe and the title of a Divine Guru?" asked Seva.

"Be prepared to be labeled crazy. In the West, the corporate Gurus refer to far flung ideas as thinking outside the box. Something becomes believable and is accepted only when "proved" by scientific theories and research. Tell a Westerner that their period of suffering is due to the laws of Karma and you most likely will be greeted with a blank stare, a polite smile and a nod followed by a quick exit. Tell them that the number which is derived when the date and month of birth is added and reduced to a single digit is a mathematical predictor of behavior, attitudes and destiny and once again, most likely, you will be met with a blank stare. To Easterners, for instance, nine is a crazy number. It is the highest of nine digits and thus this number acts like it is God. When placed in a circle, it thinks that it is a complete zero and tries to act that way. Not knowing what it really is makes it act in confusion. In the world of true mathematics the number 9 added to any number will result in the same basic number."

"I don't understand, my Guru," said Seva.

"Well if you add 9 + 3 you will get 12 but when the digits in 12 is added it becomes 3 again." If 9 is multiplied by 3 it also becomes 9 again by adding the 2 and 7 in 27."

"That is amazing!," said Seva excitedly.

"9 has a mysterious relationship with all the other numbers," said the Guru with a smile.

"What do you mean?"

"Well, slow down for a minute now. Let us look at some really crazy ideas before we venture to 'crazy nines'."

"Don't you mean 'crazy eights'?" asked Seva humorously.

"My point exactly. In 1956, at age six, a child was walking home from school at 3 o'clock in the hot tropical sun. He stopped to rest under the shade of a sour-sop tree by the roadside and looked down to find himself standing on a rectangular patch of sod about six feet by three feet. He thought, 'would it not be nice if this patch of earth can be made to move and transport tired folk from one place to the next?

This thought originated in the mind of a six-year old, born into poverty in a small farming village in the backwaters of a third-world nowhere, where television was unknown and radios were owned by city folk, none of whom ever venture into poor villages. Two decades later, when that twenty-six-year old set foot on civilized soil, he stepped unto an escalator which gave him a ride from point A to point B."

"Wow," exclaimed Seva.

"Let me give you another example," Guruji said, with a faraway look in his eyes. Seva, also his devotee did not have the heart to say 'no' although he knew he would be late for work.

"Desmond Tutu, the South African priest, once told a humorous story about the spread of Christianity in the third world. The white man came into the village and as all the villagers gathered around him, the white man ordered everyone to close their eyes and kneel in prayer. When the poor villagers opened their eyes, each one of them had a Bible in their hand. The white man had their land."

"I don't understand."

"The villagers didn't either. Anyways, the white English army folk eventually taught the villagers to plant crops in neat rows dig drainage canals in straight lines and build homes with concrete blocks and zinc sheets imported from England, the king pin of the Great British Empire. By this time the 'escalator lad' was eighteen [1+8=9]. He began to wonder why it was so uncomfortable to sleep at nights. He thought how wonderfully cool it would be to have a thatched roof hut built with mud walls with a lizard on the ceiling to keep away flies and other tropical insects. The natural materials will keep the inside cool and comfortable. He mentioned his brilliant idea to this class. Everyone, including his teacher, had a hearty laugh and labeled him as crazy."

"And this was the same teacher, I bet, who wore a necktie and a suit jacket in 90-degree tropical heat."

"I think you are beginning to get the point, my student. One final example: At twenty-seven [2+7=9] the 'escalator lad' began to come under the influence of the 'civilized' world. His first child was two years old. One evening as he sat in the sparsely furnished apartment with a brand new television set, he was overcome by a single thought. He looked at his son staring intently at the television images. It was if the child was mesmerized. At that moment in time, he thought that television cannot be a healthy thing. He asked his wife if they could get rid of it. In the ensuing family debate, he gave up and his only son was left to the influence of the magical influence of the television screen. Through that medium, that child developed his sense of self. It is now twenty-seven years later and critical educators have been increasingly talking, especially over the last five years, about the media influence on the development of children's lives. At twenty-seven, that child, now with his own child growing up, is just beginning to un-yoke himself from the clutches of popular media. Years of that child's life was lost, my student. And for what? For a few hundred people to get rich and fuel their insatiable ego. It is really very simple, my student. At the heart of the nine lies the mystery that governs the well-being of human existence. How many digits are there?"

"Nine."

"The cat has ….?"

"Nine lives."

"There are nine forms of light energy. There are nine forms of Laxmi, the Hindu Goddess of Light. Nine planets influence the weather, the rise and fall of the oceans, our daily lives and more."

"I see."

"The official residence of the President of the United States of America is the White House at Number 1600 (which equals 7) Pennsylvania Avenue. What does that prove? Let me add another complexity for you. The house number in which OJ Simpson lived was nine. Nicole Brown Simpson was murdered at a Number Six, the upside down nine. The murder at Virginia Tech was in room #207 (2+7=9)."

"The number nine does seem to be a high profile digit indeed."

"Yes my student, it is. The present mathematical Base 10 system, presented in circle of the universe, places the Number Nine [9] between One [1] and Zero [0]. The ninth lunar day occurs when the sun and moon are farthest from each other. People born on this day experience confusion since they are born on that thin line between Cosmic Reality and deep Spirituality. In other words, such persons are between what is traditionally known as Heaven and Hell and the pull from each side results in the confusion. When such persons live in a location where the House Number is also a nine, instead of harmony, total disharmony results with destructive effects such as murders, family breakups, frequent quarrels, criminal activities, disobedient children. The house lot number nine correlates with the natural order of the universe; in other words, the number allotted to a particular location is the result of the consciousness of the universe and is the point where the positive and negative energies meet. Remember that the universe is a living entity. Each object has a history and a memory which is an accumulation of all information pertaining to that object throughout its history.

Since the numbering and measurements under the Base 10 rule is harmonic, we all tend to see things in the same way. A change in the Base of the mathematical measurement system will enable us to conceive the future in this present moment and depending upon the new Base, a person will be able to transcend different dimensions within a moment of time. This is nothing new. The sages and Rishis in the Himalayas have been 'traveling' this way for thousands of years. Proving this to the Western world is akin to Newton 'proving' the existence of gravity. Before the apple fell on Newton's head, did gravity not exist in the universe?"

Seva took the blessings from his guru and slowly, but thoughtfully rose from his position at the feet of Guruji Sri Swami Ram who continued to sit in the lotus position under the shade of the huge banyan tree near the Florida Everglades.

Seva hesitated for a brief moment and adjusted the straps on his knapsack. He looked over at his Guru and saw his eyes were closed in meditation.

"Yes student?"

Seva was accustomed to his master's insight by now and nothing surprised him anymore. It was as if his Guru could read his thoughts.

"Well, I often ponder what people seek from life. Some are very happy when they are in positions of authority, others when they can show off their wealth and power. It seems that material success creates happiness."

"Material success does create happiness. It is the abuse of material success which results in human suffering. One of our future lessons will be on the laws of Karma. For now, let us concentrate on happiness. There are really five aspects of happiness. You are familiar with Mazlow's hierarchy of needs, are you not?"

"Yes. Mazlow postulated that after Man has fulfilled the basic need of food, shelter and protection, he seeks out more and more from life until he reaches what is called Self Actualization."

"Exactly. The hierarchy of needs follow a logical pathway. In a similar way, the five aspects of happiness follow a very logical pathway. For instance, if a study group or any sample of people were asked to complete the following sentence, 'Happiness to me means _____' each one is likely to write something slightly different, but the general thrust of the answers will be similar. To approach the concept of happiness in a different way, let us reflect for a moment, on the opposite concept. The concept of un-happiness. Essentially, we become unhappy when we do not get what we want. We become frustrated, anxious, angry, hateful or any combination thereof. It is at this point, most of us begin to reflect on wholesomeness of our inner being because we recognize that something is wrong in our lives. In other words, we begin to seek out happiness.

According to the ancient Vedic scriptures, [Garud Purana V1. Ch 115.20] the five-fold aspects of happiness comprise:

1. Remunerative knowledge

2. Companionship of the good.

3. Freedom from sickness.

4. A loving spouse.

5. Obedient children.

Do you see the logical flow?"
"Yes, Guruji"

"I know you are getting anxious about being late for work. Please leave now. Your boss is being delayed by the accident on the Turnpike."

Seva turned quickly with an anxious look on his face.

"No, No. She is not injured. She was not involved in the accident."

Relieved, Seva turned and walked out from under the shade of the banyan tree.

CHAPTER 1

What are equations of life?

Even though Swami Sri Bharat Tirth Raj brought out this knowledge of Vedic Mathematics in the 1940's, the actual science of Vedic mathematics was noted long before that. In fact it is the basis for the creation of the world as well as the Hindu culture and sociological formation of the Indian Vedic sciences, which is also the foundation of religious science of Hinduisms; even now practiced today. It is from this mathematical science that all other sciences were developed. Here in this book I will show you that "God does not play dice with the world" as Einstein had said. There really is a mathematical system in the formation of the universe that can explain all of life.

This simply can be proven by the science of Vedic mathematics. It also will prove that the knowledge and science of mathematics was lost and when rediscovered by the modern masters such as Pythagoras, or Arybatha and so on, they left out the spiritual application of mathematics. Their discoveries were made up from pieces of lost information found in ancient texts left over by the sages and seers. Hence short division become long division, short multiplication became long multiplication, and so on. This process of putting the process of original Vedic Mathematical equations together resulted in our lost view of the world as we should see it and so the view of true reality became limited

With the help of Vedic mathematics and *Life Code* Science, I will show that Vedic mathematics can provide a thoughtful process that will change the way we look at reality. Mankind will be able to make wonderful progress into the future with more powerful visions and knowledge of the universe.

This book is not in any way or form suggesting that our present mathematical system is absolute or inefficient in anyway. In fact, the presentation in this book will enhance our present mathematical system. We will be able to actually enjoy mathematics in a whole different light. With this new improvement to our present mathematic system scientific progress will reach new levels of application and benefits to the human race.

Life Code and the *Equation of Life* courses offer you this opportunity to understand your own reality as well as others. If all things in the universe were coded without flaw, then there would be a unique system whereby an equation could be developed that explains how to exactly go about achieving a happy, well planned, successful life. The *Equation of Life* course provides these equations and answers all questions that come up in life so as to help you find your definition of happiness.

THE MORE YOU KNOW...THE MORE YOU WILL SEE...

AND THE MORE PROSPEROUS YOU WILL BE

If simple equations could answer life's most complicated problems, then would it not benefit people greatly in the world? If a mother can know instantly at birth what her child would be like as he/she grows up, would that not be helpful for her to steer the child's life in a more successful way? If a young child can know which career path to follow for personal satisfaction and life long success, would that not bring more happiness to the child as well as the society we live in? These and more are the benefits of the *Life Code* Sciences that originated from Ancient Vedic Sciences.

When I discovered how easy it was to perform complicated calculations within seconds using the ancient science of Vedic Mathematics, I realized that western mathematics was missing a lot of something, which I did not quite understand. Nevertheless I continued my studies in comparing western sciences to Eastern sciences and as I got deeper in my studies, I realized that the knowledge of how the universe works has been discovered many thousands of years ago. In other words, the questions we all ask about our life have all been answered already. Except in the process of Time and Man's ego, those answers have been lost as mankind lost its mental pursuits and lusted after material possessions.

Imagine how wonderful life would be if with a simple number, one can measure material as well as spiritual or conscious energies. Using a basic calculation of addition, one can determine all their experiences with a partner, a car or the house he/she lives in. One can even understand all about their love problems and solutions and therefore, can solve them. All these amazing revelations came to me slowly as I did my research and development in the ancient Vedic Mathematics of the Universe. I realized at an early stage in my research that I have discovered the Equations of Life.

A mind boggling realization took place when I discovered the equations of my own life and saw that everything from my own past, present and future could be calculated by a simple equation. This began an exciting journey for me in the field of Vedic Sciences, Quantum Physics and the theories behind Mathematics and Philosophy. A path that seems to be so profound, that the depth cannot be measured. This book offers you that number and equation. An equation and number you will never forget after reading this book!

CHAPTER 2

Equation #1 - Your Lifecode –
Who Are You?

ADD THE MONTH AND DAY OF YOUR BIRTH TOGETHER. THE RESULT IS YOUR LIFECODE YOUR LIFE CODE REVEALS ALL YOUR EXPERIENCES AND YOUR PERSONALITY

To find your own personal *Life Code*, the following table has been provided. Each birth date from January 1 to December 31 is included in the table. Against each month and day of birth, you will find the Life Code that matches that day of birth. For example, if you were born August 15th, your *Life Code* is 5. This number or code will be referred to as your LIFECODE.

TABLE #1- LIFE CODES

	YOUR DAY OF BIRTH								
YOUR	1	2	3	4	5	6	7	8	9
MONTH	10	11	12	13	14	15	16	17	18
OF	19	20	21	22	23	24	25	26	27
BIRTH	28	29	30	31					
JANUARY	2	3	4	5	6	7	8	9	1
FEBRUARY	3	4	5	6	7	8	9	1	2
MARCH	4	5	6	7	8	9	1	2	3
APRIL	5	6	7	8	9	1	2	3	4
MAY	6	7	8	9	1	2	3	4	5
JUNE	7	8	9	1	2	3	4	5	6
JULY	8	9	1	2	3	4	5	6	7
AUGUST	9	1	2	3	4	5	6	7	8
SEPTEMBER	1	2	3	4	5	6	7	8	9

OCTOBER	2	3	4	5	6	7	8	9	1
NOVEMBER	3	4	5	6	7	8	9	1	2
DECEMBER	4	5	6	7	8	9	1	2	3

Your Life Based on *Life Code*#1

- You are independent, lonely sometimes and like to be in charge.
- You will achieve high status in career and position in life.
- You are very spiritual in your thinking and you think constantly.
- You are bossy and commanding in your actions toward others.
- You were very lonely and independent as a child.
- You always feel that others leave you alone a great deal.
- In marriage you should not be too assertive or your independence may result in your partner leaving you for another.
- You worry a great deal and this may result in mental nervousness.

As the first number, this represents the origin, the solitary eminence of the Sun, the creator. It is a powerful and creative number, associated with strong masculinity, and people bearing it may become leaders. It refers very much to the self, so people who have it will be individuals with a tendency to be inventive, determined, and possessed of a pioneering spirit. Along with such power must go responsibility, and unless the person is careful, there is a risk of falling into selfishness, egotism, and severe bossiness. If their schemes fail, they may become aggressive or introverted; even if their schemes succeed, they may become overbearing and ruthless.

At the time of birth, one of your parents was promoted to a leadership position. As a child you were left alone a great deal and may have experienced loneliness being away from your parents. You are a very independent person who does not like to follow others' advice unless it is beneficial to you. Most of the time you like to do your own thing. You may be very controlling and moody. You are unable to follow orders easily and may lead most of your life as a single person. You enjoy being alone sometimes and will specifically take time to contemplate on your opportunities and your emotions. You strive very hard to achieve a high position in career opportunities.

You are willing to study a great deal and may become very dominating in your home. You are required to avoid letting this dominant characteristic affect your relationship as it could result in your being divorced or separated from your lover. If you are unable to submit yourself willingly to be loved by others, your love life may be one of emptiness. Avoid taking people for granted and expecting people to follow your commands. This is a mistake and may create much unhappiness in your life. If you were born at an inauspicious time without proper consultations with priests you may experience much loneliness in life and rejection by all.

Your Life Based on *Life Code#2*

- You like to shop a great deal and specifically look for bargains.
- You are a great cook and will make a great chef at any restaurant.
- Any dishes prepared by you will be tasty to others.
- You are advised to always serve food to reap good karma.
- Feeding anyone who visits your home will bless you with prosperity.
- You do not like to deal with work that involves too many calculations.
- You have a kind heart and are very helpful to others...sometimes too much.
- Others may take advantage of your kindness.
- You are a very religious person.
- You have a great voice and may become a famous singer.
- Marriage may become difficult as a result of illicit affairs.
- You receive a great deal of love, but cannot give it.
- You are not romantic but like to be romanced by your beloved.

Just as #1 is associated with maleness, so #2 is with femininity, being gentle, intuitive, harmonious and romantic. It is symbolized by the Moon and suggests a mental creativity and an ability to mix well with other people, but an inability to be forceful, to make decisions, or to carry tasks to their necessary conclusions; more mental power than physical.

You are a kind and generous individual and very true in your feelings for others. You like to assist those that are distressed or those who need help genuinely. You have very few enemies and you are loved by many. Normally according to previous karma, you should be happily married, have a romantic lifestyle and be a dedicated homemaker. These individuals must be properly matched to those individuals born under Life Code 5, 8 or 1. You are a very cooperative person and will work easily with others. If you are a woman, you are extremely romantic in your love life and very emotional when it comes to being deceived by others. You are very self-sacrificing and can be an ideal spouse. You love the world and would like to give a lot of yourself to the world.

In your career you may become very popular and well known by your community. You are a good cook and will enjoy others in this way. You are advised not to let your ego dominate your personality as this may create great conflicts in your life. Always try to be humble and spiritual. Usually if you are spiritual, all your wishes are granted in life. You do not wish to be extremely rich but you do require a comfortable lifestyle. Hindus, who are suffering marriage problems, should attend meditation classes, learn how to be humble and pay respects to elders and priests in their community. For prosperity in life, you should always offer something to drink or eat to any person visiting your home. Christians should humble themselves and be more charitable to the church and the community to ward off any negative influences.

Your Life Based on *Life Code*#3

- You may be very skinny and small in stature with a thin waist.
- You are very argumentative and usually think you are right.
- You may experience loss of children or abortions in your life.
- If woman, you may experience problems with your uterus.
- You may also experience cramps or lower back pain.
- You are childish in your ways...people think you are immature.
- You hesitate to accept responsibility.

- You may have many children.
- You may be involved in publishing, writing or selling books.
- Your career may involve some form of communication.

Threes are creative and disciplined people, associated with the planet Jupiter. Growth, success, luck, happiness and fertility are suggested, though on the negative side the person may also be gossipy, moody, overcritical, sometimes rather shy or pessimistic or unimaginative and prone to leaving jobs half done. You will fare especially well with other 3s.

Usually you are a very jovial and happy person. In most cases your ego will not allow others to upset you or prevent you from achieving your desires or your satisfaction to be right always. You are very youthful looking and even in old age will look 10 years younger than you really are. You may have a petite body and enjoy such hobbies as dancing, music and swimming. You express yourself very clearly to others and may be asked to give speeches to groups of people. You love children and would very much like to have them around you. Children enjoy your company because you are very playful. Other adults may find you immature at times and in love relationships your partner may think you are very childish in your ways.

If you are negative you may be denied the opportunity of having children. If such is the case, a Religious Guru may be very helpful to you. You like to read a great deal and can be a good communicator. You may spend a great deal of your time on the phone.

A career associated with electronic communication may be very beneficial to you. Those who are educated may find themselves wanting to publish or write books as you make an excellent author. If you are not religious, your negativity may present you with many difficulties in life that may create great losses through younger people. Also you may experience the sickness of children around you. Christians are advised to meditate on Jesus Christ as a teacher and on the words "The Lord is my shepherd and I am the sheep."

Your Life Based on *Life Code*#4

- You are very hardworking and conscientious.
- You have a high temper and may experience many stressful moments.

- You are very determined in your attitude and will not admit defeat easily.
- If you want something, you are determined to have it at any cost.
- Your health may be affected by too much work.
- You will do very well in life if you own a home.
- Real estate investments are very lucky for you.

There is completeness in 4, because mathematically it is a square. It is associated with the Earth and its 4 seasons, and people under its influence tend to be very down to Earth, systematic, practical and stable, upholding law and order, and using logic and reason in their actions. Yet there is also an earthbound and unimaginative side to these people, who may be over-fussy about small details, lazy, weak and prone to worrying too much. Occasionally, a 4 will have a stubborn, rebellious streak. Friendship is difficult.

You are an extremely hard-working person and sometimes people refer to you as a workaholic. You are very slow and methodical in your actions. It is very hard for someone to get you to change your mind once you have made a decision. And even if you do agree to comply you may experience difficulty adapting to the change or anything new in life. You are very dutiful in your home and may be found to be constantly doing something around the house.

You make an excellent carpenter and may be very successful in the field of construction. As a contractor you may become very wealthy in life. You are a collector of antiques or articles of memory. You may be the owner of many homes or none if you are negative. You may also be a landlord and if you are negative may experience many troubles and court problems with tenants. You may acquire properties through inheritance from your parents or a dead relative. If you are employed in a business of your own you may be working more hours than you really get compensated for. If you are in a regular job, you may be asked to put in a lot of overtime.

If you are negative, your most major problems in life may be related to your career. Laziness may definitely bring you down to poverty and ruin. You are advised to avoid placing yourself under too much pressure or tension as this may create high blood pressure problems. Avoid overwork and lifting heavy equipment. If you are not an attorney you may experience delays and problems through attorneys. You may experience rheumatic pains in your joints.

If you are a positive person, you may settle down into a very comfortable and large home, well decorated and taken care of by your spouse. Christians are advised to study the experiences of Abraham in the Old Testament.

Your Life Based on *Life Code#5*

- You change your mind a great deal and very quickly.
- You love to travel and will experience many changes of residence.
- It is very hard for others to access your thinking.
- You have great intuitive powers and will usually know things ahead of time.
- You can read another's personality very easily.
- You can feel the energy of others and may know their thoughts about you.
- Usually you are too helpful to others to the detriment of yourself...you give too much of yourself.
- You do many things to help others without asking for compensation.
- Your connection with the Universe is very profound and your mission in life seems to be to help others.
- You give great counseling and advice to friends and family.
- You are not very lucky with relative and family members.
- You make friends easily...friends help you the most in life.
- The more good actions in life, the more beneficial it will be for you.
- You have the ability to develop psychic powers and heal others by touching.
- You may experience problems with the government, IRS or immigration.
- At some point in your life you will be influenced greatly by a spiritual leader.

Five represents the senses. There is activity, change, hatred of routine, need for novelty and a reputation for unpredictability. These people are energetic, adaptable, resourceful, intelligent and quick to learn. They may demand too much of others, be too impulsive, and spread themselves too thin with too many projects at once. They make friends very easily, but are difficult to live with.

Sex, romance, lust, beauty and physical satisfaction are some of the qualities in your life. You are very much attracted to the opposite sex and you, yourself, may be quite a handsome or beautiful person. You may be easily tempted into having illicit affairs if your willpower is weak. On the other hand individuals like you can become the perfect husband or wife. If you find the right spouse you will be extremely faithful. The right spouse in this case means that he or she must be romantic and an extremely willing and skilled lover. If these qualities are present in your marriage everything else falls into place.

You will enjoy traveling and may visit many places in your life. You can bring change to a lot of people's lives and are sometimes great advisers to others but not to yourself. Wherever you are present some change may occur. It is also possible that with proper knowledge and guidance you may bring about enormous changes to world philosophy and thinking. You are a great writer and can tell convincing short stories that may change people's beliefs. It is also possible that you may change your residence many times in your life and may live mostly away from your birthplace.

Your greatest downfall can be lust or sexual indulgences. If you are negative you may want to make love to every member of the opposite sex you come into contact with. Your taste for music can be of a wide variety and you may be concerned mostly with satisfying your bodily needs rather than your mental needs. If you are positive, you may become and extremely skilled businessman or politician and may achieve very wealthy and successful positions in life. At some point in your life you may be accused falsely by others and may be stuck with many debts and loans with you may not be able to repay. You are the carrier of good news or bad news and may even like to gossip or involve yourself in informative conversations. To enjoy this karma you must learn to be sincere in all your actions. Be religious and be respectful to elders and keep an open mind.

Your Life Based on *Life Code#6*

- You like to be in charge and have a very strong ego.
- You may experience a career with many responsibilities, which you may handle well.
- If you fail to handle your responsibilities in life you will experience misery.
- You may experience lower or upper back pain...if not, headaches or migraines.
- A bad diet may affect your blood pressure and health.
- If you are not working for the government, you may be constantly harassed due to problems with the government.
- If you are having a difficult time repaying your debts, you could lose your home through foreclosure.
- You may be very responsible and have a business of your own.
- You do not accept astrology or occult studies very easily.
- You feel very frustrated, especially when you cannot have things your way.
- Your key to happiness is acceptance and spirituality.
- You should avoid the color red; it creates pain.

Six is the number of the emotions. Mathematically, 6 is a "perfect number" because it is the sum of its factors, 1, 2, and 3. People under its sway tend to be reliable and well rounded. There is love of home, peace, beauty, and harmony. Sixes tend to be artistic and good with children and animals. They may also be too sympathetic, too self-sacrificing, too stubborn, too concerned with duty, perhaps too interfering. But they are among the most popular of people, making good friends and partners.

Responsibility, high tempers and power are some of the qualities in your life. It is possible that as a young person growing up you possessed a very strong personality and a high temper. You may have many quarrels with relatives and friends because of jealousy or a battle for power. You like to be in charge and are not willing to take orders from others very easily. You prefer to be a supervisor or boss instead of an employee. Your ego is very high and this may present many difficulties in your life where you may be unable to admit that you are wrong even when you know you are.

If you are negative, it is quite possible that you may suffer from serious pain in your lower back for which doctors are unable to find a cure. You should see the Hindu priest or astrologer for proper advice on how to get rid of this back pain, which can be very irritating sometimes. In addition to this affliction you may also suffer migraine headaches, which may result from your inability to control your inner anger.

If positive and religious, you can make out to be an excellent marriage partner provided you assume proper responsibility for your family and relationships. You are accident-prone and must be careful when handling machinery or vehicles. Employment with the government or the military forces may be very beneficial to you and you are advised to seek such opportunities. On the other hand, you enjoy power and dominion over your life and your environment.

As a leader or supervisor you perform excellently and earn respect from others. If you allow your ego to make you a non-believer in religion or god, you may suffer prolonged diseases such as high blood pressure, heart problems or cancer. These diseases may develop as a result of constantly eating meat, drinking alcohol or taking unnecessary drugs. It is advisable for you to be vegetarian if possible and maintain a meditation schedule. For other non-believers it is possible that you may experience many difficulties with the courts, attorneys and mortgage companies. You must learn to maintain your responsibility with regard to loans or any monies borrowed.

Married individuals may experience many separations from their spouses, possibly as a result of unexpected responsibilities, which may create misunderstandings. People, who are usually divorced as a result of this, may find themselves very unhappy after the divorce for their wealth and prosperity lies in staying married. Christians are advised to read the book of Proverbs and follow the advice given there for worship of the Lord.

Your Life Based on *Life Code*#7

- Your mind is running at a thousand miles an hour.
- You are constantly thinking and analyzing everything.

- Sometimes you keep most of your thoughts to yourself.
- You do not tell your plans very easily to others.
- You feel you are right in everything 99% of the time.
- Sometimes you think everyone is against you.
- If woman, you are very beautiful or, if male, handsome.
- You attract the opposite sex very easily.
- Your need for love and romance is very high.
- You experience many difficulties in your marriage.
- A sure key to happiness for you is meditation and music.
- You are kind hearted and can be deceived easily by your lovers.
- You should avoid the color black; wear light colors.

Seven is the most significant and magical of the numbers. It has long been held sacred, as is shown by the extraordinary frequency of 7 in mythology, the Bible, and classifications of all kinds. There are 7 notes in the musical scale, 7 phases of the Moon, 7 seas, 7 heavenly bodies in the old Ptolemaic system, 7 wonders of the ancient world, 7 hills of Rome, 7 virtues, 7 deadly sins, 7 days of creation, 7 plagues of Egypt, 7 sentences in the Lord's Prayer, 7 trumpets in the Apocalypse, and many more. The 7th son of a 7th son is believed to possess great magical powers.

People who are 7s are sometimes great thinkers and may have an occult or psychic side. They may be researchers, investigators or inventors. They have an affinity with the sea and often travel widely. But they must use their powers wisely, avoiding pride and cynicism and accepting that their talents will never make them materially rich.

You have a very secretive and sometimes very private personality. You hardly speak what you are thinking but your mind is running at 100 miles per hour. However, when you do speak, your words are like fire ready to destroy the person you are speaking to. People around you see you as an eggshell ready to break with the slightest intimidation, so your partner or lover feels like he or she is always walking on eggshells because he or she never knows when you are going to find something wrong with him or her. Your criticism of others can be very high and may prevent others from getting very close to you. You tend to hold back a lot of your personal feelings for others. Even your beloved will ask you when are you going to say, "I love you"? It is very important that you do not analyze others too much for no one is perfect in everything. The first lesson you must learn in life is that no one can be perfect. Once you have learned this, your love life and your marriage life will be much happier.

You possess a very high temper and may sometimes speak very harshly to others. If this quality is carried into your marriage it may end in divorce. Out of all others in this astrological analysis you possess the highest ego there is. You will never admit when you are wrong. You will never admit when you feel weak inside, and you will always put up an outward appearance much different from the inner one. Your true feelings never seem to come out, even though your true feelings given to the other person would solve all the problems.

If you are an extremely negative individual, you may be addicted to drugs, alcohol or smoking. You may also be constantly complaining over petty or unnecessary matters. A small matter may worry you a great deal. You are constantly studying or reading if you are not sleeping or relaxing watching TV. You are very slow in your movements and may experience many delays in your life as a result of this.

You may get married very late in life. If you do get married early there may be a possibility of separation. Late marriages are usually more successful. Your interests may lie in the field of medicine, and if you study medical sciences you will be successful in a career associated with it. If you are a positive individual you may become a priest, a yogi or saint. If you are religious you may experience inner encounters with God and other divine manifestations of the universal deities. If you happen to find yourself a guru, you may experience a divine connection through that personality. If this path is followed, most of your wishes will be fulfilled in life and your desires may become a reality. You may encounter many religious individuals in your life. You are advised to pay much attention to what they say for their advice may be very beneficial to you. Respect must be given to all holy people or elders in the family. Christians are advised to say the Lord's Prayer 11 times every day.

Your Life Based on *Life Code#8*

- You love money and constantly think about it.
- You may have a business of your own.
- Money flows through your hands very easily.
- If you are spiritual and conservative, money will stay.
- You love expensive things and may shop a lot.
- Your favorite color may be pink if you are female.
- You have a strong ego.
- Investment in stocks may prove profitable.
- You love jewelry and may own of lot of it.
- Avoid wearing anything black, as it will kill your prosperity.
- Silver and pearl are very lucky for you and will make you prosperous.

These people will achieve success but not necessarily happiness. They may possess the drive and ability to lead, and thus receive material wealth and recognition, but they can often drive themselves too hard, repressing their feelings, suffering tension, and missing out on satisfying relationships.

All of your actions and your thoughts are related to money. You may become a wealthy businessperson or a bankrupt millionaire. You like to buy expensive and extravagant items. Your taste is very luxurious and your thinking is very materialistic. You worry a great deal about money and may be a big spender or a big saver according to your karma in this life. You may experience sudden prosperity in life and then all of a sudden find yourself in poverty again, for this is a very karmic influence that you are born under. The life that you lead now may account for all the good or bad actions you have performed in previous lives. This is called the judgment life for you. As a businessperson you may own a very large and profitable company. As an employee you may be earning a very high salary.

If you are negative you may be unable to save any money in the bank. You may also experience a great deal of financial problems and may lose money through the opposite sex. Your spending may be more than your income. Other negatives are revolution, rupture, excess materialism, deceit and trickery with regard to money and so on.

On the other hand, if you are a positive and a very spiritual person you could become very powerful and very wealthy. Your understanding of material aspects will be excellent throughout your life and you will be a very successful money earner. You are an excellent negotiator in business transactions and may achieve most of your wealth after your marriage. You possess a special ability to analyze financial trends and gambling secrets that few people may know about. If you are careful about your health and the kind of food you eat, you may live a very long life, possibly up to 108 years. You may become very wealthy through investments in real estate or stock markets.

Your sexual vitality is very high and this may present some interesting romantic adventures in your life. You seek occupations that are very political and powerful such as city manager, corporate director, etc. This power or money could well go the other way as much as its promises can be destructive. This karma is called the judgment of life where all actions from past lives are in this life are accounted for. Christians are advised to follow the parables outlined in the New Testament in the teachings of Christ and look upon him as the true Teacher of mankind.

Your Life Based on *Life Code*#9

- You may have a high temper and a suspicious mind.
- You may experience the death of very close family members.
- Take care to avoid accidents and traffic violations.
- Alcohol is very damaging to your life; avoid it.
- You think very deeply about life and may be extremely religious.
- If you are positive you may become famous.
- You make a great politician or spiritual guru.
- You will live a long life and may work in a hospital.
- Working for the government greatly benefits you.
- You seem to be always struggling to fulfill your desires in life.
- You spend more than you earn and will have financial problems.

- You are very honest and may lose in partnerships because of this.
- Negative husbands may abuse their wives physically and mentally.
- You have a loud voice and love to shout at other sometimes.
- The keys to your happiness are to attend churches and donate your time and energy to charitable organizations.

If the #1 symbolizes the beginning, the number #9 embraces all the previous numbers and symbolizes finality and completeness. Numerologically it reproduces itself, as the digits of all multiples of 9 add up to 9; for example, 4 x 9=36, then 3+6=9. It is a sacred and mystical number with many Biblical and legendary references: 9 orders of angels, a 9 days' wonder, 9 points of the law, 9 months of pregnancy, 9 lives of a cat, and so on.

Nines are determined fighters; they tend to be compassionate, determined, seekers after perfection, but also self-regarding, impulsive, possessive and moody. Their friendships tend to be with 3s and 6s. Sometimes you doubt the existence of God and sometimes you believe in God. You are a child of the sea and must pray to the ocean for the fulfillment of your desires.

Your temper, your passions and your inner self are constantly erupting like a volcano. If you are positive you may experience a highly spiritual or psychic connection with the Universe. You could become very famous in life and will make an excellent priest or Brahmin. A positive involvement with the government may put you in the position of a police officer, congressman or even president of a country. A negative involvement with the government may bring you into association with criminals, accusation of a crime or in conflict with the courts, the IRS or lawyers.

You are very high natured and usually need the companion of the opposite sex constantly. After marriage your frustrations can easily result in aggressiveness if you are denied sexual attention from your lover. Even though you are aware that you are wrong in many things, you may deny that such things are happening to you and this usually results in negative attractions to life.

If you are negative, you may become an alcoholic or a drug addict. This type of life may surely bring you into contact with the courts and the prisons. Your harshness to others and your temper must be controlled; otherwise you may experience divorces, violent encounters with your spouse or lover and possible exposure to distress from criminals.

On the other hand, if you are positive you may experience many unique religious psychic and astrological experiences. You could become very famous or notorious. It is possible that you may experience misfortune and accidents in the middle part of your life. If you are negative and insult or criticize religious groups or individuals, you may receive a curse from God. This may come in the form of cancer, AIDS, tuberculosis or any other incurable diseases. Your karma in this life is to read, learn, meditate, teach and learn the wisdom of life. Some of you may become hermits, yogis and gurus prepared to save the world from sin and destruction. Your knowledge is very high and encompassing. You could develop a great love for others without boundaries. You usually experience the death of many friends and family. Your home may also be located close to a cemetery or a large body of water. You may also experience natural disasters such as hurricanes and earthquakes, etc.

Your life may change every nine years and, depending upon whether it is positive or negative, the change may follow accordingly. You have the ability to request from god directly all the things you desire in life. However this can be done only if you maintain positive relationship with the government, peaceful love life with your spouse and respectful humility with elders and priests. Even if you are a judge and you have violated the divine principles of life, you may be struck down. The only way to achieve success in your life is to meditate, seek out a teacher and maintain a strict meatless diet. You must always be ready to follow the philosophy of truth and be willing to teach or give without selfishness. Christians are advised to fast and regularly attend church services and do charitable work.

CHAPTER 3

Equation #2 – Why Were You Born? (Your Purpose)

ADD THE LIFE CODE # TO THE YEAR OF BIRTH AND AFTER REDUCING TO SINGLE DIGIT NUMBER THE RESULT IS YOU LIFE PATH CODE

Eg: Add Feb 12, 1956 as 2 +1+2+1+9+5+6 = 26 → 2 + 6 = 8 – Life path code is #8

Your Purpose in Life Based on Life Path Code #1

When born under this Life Path Code and following a negative path, you must learn to fall back on your own resources (i.e. your strength and your knowledge) and make your own decisions. You must work on your inner self – mind, body and spirit. You must learn to be original and to establish new ideas, new ideals and new tactics. Try to break away from the standard trends and be your own person.

Perhaps the most important lesson for you to learn is that there are other people in the world besides you. You must learn to live with others without bullying or imposing unjustly your own will power upon them. If you follow a positive path, you will find your way open for positive action and achievement.

Individual action, originality, new creations, progress and ambition are some dominant things in your life. You will possess self-confidence, assurance and pride; your life will be filled with activity. This Life Path Code indicates that you will usually be able to stand on your own feet and have the desire to be your own person as opposed to being involved with associates or partners.

Learn to be independent. Do not take advantage of others. Be a leader. Be spiritual. Enjoy being alone. Take time to meditate.

Your Purpose in Life Based on Life Path Code #2

When born under this Life Path Code and following a negative path, the keyword is subservience. The lesson that you must learn is not to put yourself before others. You must learn cooperation, patience and consideration for others. Learn to overcome shyness and over-sensitivity. When following a positive path, you will find a life full of cooperation, the ability to work well with others and to follow instructions.

This will be a life full of gentle love and peace, for the karma of this Life Path Code is to give and to seek love and companionship. Your best role is peacemaker but be aware because unscrupulous people can take advantage of the kindness of people in this form.

Be cooperative. Avoid being too kind. Marry only once. Avoid divorce. Don't be too materialistic. Take care with your words, and do not be too outspoken to others.

Your Purpose in Life Based on Life Path Code #3

When born under this Life Path Code and following a negative path, the lesson you must learn is self-expression, to give freely of the self and to share your feelings openly, without fear. One of the biggest dangers you must overcome is that of jealousy. When following the positive path, consider yourself fortunate, for this is the nicest of all codes to have.

This is the code of self-expression in the way of peaceful, enjoyable activities surrounded by beauty, inner peace and harmonious atmosphere. This code will lead to many friends and companions. It will be a life of inspiration, talent and kindness.

Read and write a lot. Avoid childlessness. Accept all responsibilities in life. Avoid abortions and laziness. Learn to bow to all people of authority.

Your Purpose in Life Based on Life Path Code #4

When born with this Life Path Code and following a negative path, you must be able to use your ability to apply yourself to detail work. You must learn to stay put, become the cornerstone and devote yourself in duty to your family community and country. A particular danger to overcome is that of unjust hatred. You must learn to cooperate with your spouse, as every little thing that happens to people born under this form can irritate them easily.

When following a positive path, you might still find it a difficult code to live under, as it predicts a life of hard work and effort. The outstanding qualities of this code are the abilities of organization, devotion, dignity, trust and loyalty. Under this code, you will find great responsibility because of your outstanding qualities and will confer a wide range of trust, many times unwanted.

Work hard. Listen to your employers. Avoid stress. Save your money. Avoid gambling, investments, and shady (unclear) deals. Do not be too harsh in your judgment of others.

Your Purpose in Life Based on Life Path Code #5

If you were born under this Life Path Code and are following a negative path, your keyword is freedom. You must learn to change your thoughtlessness and be ready to accept frequent, unwanted changes. Drinking habits, narcotics, sensuality and sex can be deadly if overindulged.

If following a positive path, you might still find this Life Path Code to be a difficult but varied one to live under. You will experience frequent changes in all aspects of your life in which there will be much variety and travel. You will have freedom, curiosity, adventure, aloneness and progress. Above all, your life will be the center of constant change.

Watch your back. Avoid secret love affairs. Traveling is a must. Be careful whom you trust. Help others willingly. Do not be too narrow-minded. Listen to others.

Your Purpose in Life Based on Life Path Code #6

If born under this Life Path Code and following a positive path, you will find that it leads to glory and greatness. Many people born under this code have been held back from their destinies because of negative aspects. The greatest problem you face is adjusting to circumstances and accepting things for their true value without looking for perfection in everything. Adjustment is the key word, particularly concerning domestic relationships. You must develop a willingness to serve family, friends and country. You must learn to serve without using tyranny.

If following a positive path, you may realize a quick assent to power and greatness in the material, military or political worlds. It will be a life of responsibility and service and very much the path of adjustments.

If you follow this path, you will be called upon time and time again to settle disputes, make adjustments and render final decisions. Avoid disobeying government laws and follow all traffic rules, for trouble with the police is predicted. The couple whose lives involve this Life Path Code must avoid encouraging family visitors and involvement with family affairs.

Family interference is your karma. Avoid conflicts. Be responsible. Control your anger and ego. Obey rules. Learn to follow advice of older people. Realize there are laws that need to be followed. Family is your test.

Your Purpose in Life Based on Life Path Code #7

If born under this form and following a negative path, you will create coldness towards others. You must also overcome aloofness, which results from daydreaming and mentally wandering off, for this can prevent you from performing your responsibilities. You are humiliated and embarrassed easily or embarrass others and are faithless, which can lead to disbelief in God. You must learn to go though life cheerfully accepting the problems and troubles of others.

If following a positive path, you will find this form to be that of the loner, especially with matters concerning the inner self. This is the Life Path Code of the philosopher, the deep thinker and dreamer. In this code you will find peace, spirituality, trust, faith, research and wisdom. Your life will be restful and peaceful and will not be too concerned with material things.

Learn to be independent. Don't take advantage of others. Be a leader. Be spiritual. Enjoy being alone. Learn to express your feelings openly. Do not hold back emotions. Develop your speech.

Your Purpose in Life Based on Life Path Code #8

If born under this Life Path Code and following a negative path, your key word is avoidance of greediness, jealousy and overspending. You will find that you possess a love of power and money, and power for self, intolerance, abuse and revenge. The need is to cultivate [grow] good moral business ethics and understanding of people with less force and dynamics.

If following a positive path, then this will lead you to power, authority, material and financial gains and success in all material aspects. Persons born under this form will be generous and dependable. There is outstanding inner strength and courage.

Control greed for money. Be content. Respect your mother. Control your need for luxury. Be humble. Your ego is too strong for others sometimes. Control your desire for expensive things.

Your Purpose in Life Based on Life Path Code #9

If you were born under this Life Path Code and are following a negative path, you will find the need to hold emotions in balance and your self-ego in check. A few of the pitfalls are fickleness, immortality and daydreaming. Once again, if negative, there is a possibility that you could end up in court or become a criminal. You must learn to avoid constant ego quarrels between couples and older family members and to not interfere in other's lives.

If following a positive path, then being born under this code is the all-encompassing destiny. You likely will be a world traveler and have a global outlook. You will be understanding, intuitive, knowledgeable and willing to sacrifice. You usually make marriage partners and lovers and are full of kindness and consideration. It is predicted that you would do well with a career in government agencies.

Health is your karma and it can decline if you are too suspicious, controlling and/or commanding. Believe in God at all times (not sometimes). Control your spending habits. Pay your bills first before anything else.

CHAPTER 4

Equation #3 – From Where Did You Come?

YOUR LIFE CODE NUMBER IS ALSO YOUR HEREDITARY
CODE – THE EQUATION IS YOUR MONTH AND DAY OF
BIRTH ADDED TOGETHER

Hereditary Code #1

- Your life may become lonely.
- You could become a widow or widower.
- You will have to become independent and do things for yourself.
- Your path is that of a leader and creator of things.
- With your creative ability you should invent things.
- Too many illicit affairs could make you suffer disabilities.

Hereditary Code #2

- You must lead a life of love, cooperation, embraces and willingness to do things for others.
- Marriage will be happy and comfortable.
- You will be a good cook, restaurant chef or hostess.
- Love & service to others will be your test in life.
- Being too outspoken could hurt those you love.
- Speak your heartfelt feelings with forethought.

Hereditary Code #3

- You will look younger than you are always.
- Childish in your ways, you like attention and will throw a tantrum if you do not get attention especially from partners.
- You will benefit greatly from reading, writing, teaching, babysitting or pediatrics.
- You like to listen to stories and you make a good storyteller; avoid gossiping.

Hereditary Code #4

- You will have to work very hard for your money and to achieve position in your career.
- Laziness and idleness will destroy your life.
- You will gain weight if you are lazy and do not exercise.
- You will suffer from high blood pressure and stress unless you learn to relax and eat properly after doing your tasks.

Hereditary Code #5

- You always want to believe only what you think is right.
- You always want to gain and win in anything you do for others.
- You have very sensitive skin and can experience psoriasis or skin cancer.
- You will suffer from some kind of foot problems.
- You will have difficulty in married life if your partner is not willing to bow to you and serve you.
- Sex and sexuality will be your test in life; you admire the physical forms of the opposite sex.

Hereditary Code #6

- You have a fear of separation from family and lovers.
- You get frustrated quickly which leads to anger sometimes.
- You will love power, high status and prestige in life.
- You can be unlucky with government if you are negative.
- You are a beacon to the police; you may have many traffic tickets.
- Responsibility is your test in this life – accept all tasks given.

Hereditary Code #7

- You suppress your feelings so as to avoid conflicts with others.
- Your mind is constantly analyzing and rechecking things.
- Your love life is your greatest test since you do not express love.

- You could become highly religious or an alcoholic or drug addict.
- You would make a good radio announcer or news/talk show anchor.
- You have to be careful of overindulgence and excesses.
- You could be psychic or part of a mission in life.

Hereditary Code #8

- Money, comfort and wealth are your most important priorities in this life.
- Much money will pass through your hands; control your spending.
- You like fashions and may wish to become a model or an actor.
- You like expensive things and a socially extravagant life.
- You may find yourself exchanging sexual favors for money.
- You could have a business or sales position in a large corporation.
- If you are poor, you inherited this curse from you parents.

Hereditary Code #9

- You will experience sickness, death or separation in childhood.
- You will struggle very hard to meet your goals in life.
- You will constantly go through denial about your life and God.
- You could experience court cases, imprisonment or accidents.
- You could become very famous, highly religious or notorious.
- Being spiritual and praying to the sea Gods will help you in life.
- Money spends very easily in your hands; try hard to save.
- As soon as you save a large amount, you get the urge to spend it.
- Avoid lending others money and impulsive buying habits.

CHAPTER 5

Equation #4 –
Your Spiritual Genetic Code

YOUR LIFE CODE # IS ALSO YOUR GENETIC CODE

If Your Genetic Code is #1, Then…

- Mother and father were lonely at the time of the pregnancy.
- Mother felt that she had to do a lot of chores on her own without help from anyone.
- Father was very independent and bossy.
- Mother worried a lot about her husband and felt lonely if he didn't come home early.
- Father felt independent and didn't like to be questioned by his wife constantly.

If Your Genetic Code is #2, Then…

- Mom wanted a lot of attention from Dad during the pregnancy.
- Mom was more loving to Dad during pregnancy.
- Dad use to hug Mom a lot and she missed his embraces.
- Mom was kindhearted to all and had difficulty saying no to anyone when asked for favors.
- Dad was very kind hearted and had a lot of friends when she was pregnant with you and invited them to the home a lot.
- Mom constantly took care of visitors and cooked a great deal of food for them. She shopped a lot.
- Mom liked jewelry, sweet food and getting dressed up.

If Your Genetic Code is #3, Then…

- Mom and Dad watched a lot of movies on TV and enjoyed going out to see films.
- Mom and Dad socialized a great deal and had many parties and friends.

- Mom always had a controlling effect on Dad.

If Your Genetic Code is #4, Then...

- Mom and Dad worked hard during the pregnancy.
- Mom and Dad had lots of stress over career.
- Mom and Dan experienced low pay and hard work.
- Dad had trouble with co-workers at his workplace.
- Dad experienced jealousy and competition at the job site.

If Your Genetic Code is #5, Then...

- Mom did not trust Dad during the pregnancy.
- She accused him of not being sincere with her.
- Family was not grateful or thankful to Dad and Mom.
- One parent was unfaithful and distrusting.

If Your Genetic Code is #6, Then...

- Mom had problems with the in-laws and family during pregnancy.
- There were arguments with in-laws and family members on both sides.
- Mom was frustrated with the family & in-laws.
- Mom feared losing family and attention of her husband.
- There were threats and the fear of separation between couples.
- They had police or court problems before or after birth.
- Mom and Dad ate lots of meat and struggled for power at the job.

If Your Genetic Code is #7, Then...

- Mom was very critical of Dad during the pregnancy.
- Mom was worried about Dad leaving her for someone else.
- Both Mom and Dad kept their hurtful feelings inside.
- Both Mom and Dad listened to a lot of music.
- One of them was either religious or addicted to alcohol.
- Mom was picky, particularly during her pregnancy.

If Your Genetic Code is #8, Then...

- Both Mom and Dad were worried about money and career.
- Dad might have been worried about a raise or promotion.
- Either career or business problems occupied their minds.
- Mom wanted to be a model or fashion designer or go partying.
- Dad was involved in investments of some sort and lost money.

If Your Genetic Code is #9, Then...

- Suffering, struggles and financial problems occupied the minds of the parents during the pregnancy.
- Trouble with in-laws, jealousy and suspicion were present in this pregnancy.
- Forced sexual experiences, loss of reputation and quarrels between partners affected the unborn child.
- Someone older may have died before or after the pregnancy.

CHAPTER 6

Equation #5 – The Birth Effect Code

YOUR BIRTH EFFECT CODE IS THE SAME AS YOUR LIFE CODE

If a child is born with negative qualities, it can produce a negative experience or effect on the parents who produced that child. If during pregnancy, a husband abused his wife severely, and if during his abuse, she wished him dead, then that thought will imbed itself in the unborn child's brain. If this continues to build stronger and stronger, then as the child takes birth in the physical world the reality of death can strike the husband as soon as the child sees the father.

On another view if a car is produced with inferior parts during its construction, it can kill the driver when it comes out of the factory. So the reproductive process is essential to the survival of the whole system as well as its sub-systems. We all see sometimes when a child is born, someone dies, or a parent has an accident and so on. All this can be determined by THE BIRTH EFFECT CODE.

The BIRTH EFFECT CODE is the same as the lifecode number which is the addition of the Month + Day of Birth.

Now check out some of the descriptions of life associated with THE BIRTH EFFECT CODE.

Birth Effect for Life Code #1

Your Mother and father were very lonely and had to do everything themselves – so your EFFECT to life would be one of independence and dominating

Birth Effect for Life Code #2

Mom wanted a lot of love from your Dad, but might have been denied that embrace, so your EFFECT would be one of love, kindness an co-operation with others…you have a need for love.

- 31 -

Birth Effect for Life Code #3

Mom may have lost a child before or after you, Mom and Dad were very social. Mom had children or pregnancy problems and your EFFECT would be that you will love children but would have children problems, abortions and miscarriages or have no children ever. Your uterus may be afflicted if you are a woman.

Birth Effect for Life Code #4

Both Mom and Dad worked very hard and income was low and stress was high. Because of this your EFFECT to life will be one of stress, hard work, and low earnings. You will also be very determined in your ways. Father would have job problems after your birth.

Birth Effect for Life Code #5

Mom thought about moving, and accused Dad of illicit actions, He appeared false to her and it's possible that Dad did have an affair. Because of this your EFFECT would be one of distrust in life and your will keep moving from one relationship to another or you will like traveling. Sex will become a big factor in your life as well as in your parents' life if you are an only child

Birth Effect for Life Code #6

Family troubles, Career Disagreements, Frustration and Arguments prevailed. There were thoughts of separation during your mom's pregnancy and lots of conflict with family. It's possible that your parents separated or divorced after you were born. This will be the EFFECT in your life too. You will be more successful with a second marriage or love affair. Your ego or pride is an EFFECT from your mother or father's ego. Your back pain cam from your mom's pregnancy

Birth Effect for Life Code #7

Religion, Love problems, Distress, Deep thoughts, Drugs, Alcohol, all occurred. Mom rejected your dad during pregnancy. The EFFECT of this makes you picky, particular, critical and secretive in thoughts. Your EFFECT to others love in your life will be difficult, and you can hardly express your emotional feelings to your partner.

Birth Effect for Life Code #8

Business, Money was priority; parents bought something expensive at that time. Mom was attracted to wealth and money. Dad may have had a business. The EFFECT in your life would be the same. You will be attracted to fashion, luxury, extravagance, acting, modeling and the party life.

Birth Effect for Life Code #9

Confusion, Death, Court, Sickness and conflicts all happened to Mom and Dad. The BIRTH EFFECT is highly negative. Someone may have definitely died in your family less than a year after you were born. Someone also got sick or you may have been sick yourself in childhood. You will constantly struggle to get what you want in life because your parents struggled while pregnant with you. Your BIRTH EFFECT is one of suspicion and confusion.

CHAPTER 7

Equation #6- Your Health Code

YOUR HEALTH CODE IS THE SAME AS YOUR LIFE CODE#

What kind of Health Problems a human must face in this Life? If your HEALTH CODE number is...

Health for Life Code #1

Your mind is the weakest part- Depression and Brain Illnesses are possible – diseases include mental illnesses, brain tumors, nervousness, sexual abuse

Health for Life Code #2

Your heart, your throat and your Digestive system is weak, watch what you eat...throat and esophagus problems, thyroid complaints, heart problems, feet problems

Health for Life Code #3

Your hips, womb, and sexual organs are the weakest parts. Avoid too much carbohydrates...diseases include menstrual sicknesses, childbirth problems, excessive bleeding, back pains and sexual weaknesses

Health for Life Code #4

Your back, your bones and your stomach are the weakest,. Avoid sugar, Rest a lot. Stress and diseases dealing with bones, back, leg pains, high blood pressure, and diabetes

Health for Life Code #5

Sexual Organs, your Feet and Your legs are the weakest. Circulation is important – diseases include impotence, womb problems, digestion problems, feet problems, blood circulation problems, Skin problems

Health for Life Code #6

Your back, your spine and your head are places of illness, avoid all meats. Diseases include Cancer, Tuberculosis, Surgery, Back pains, Frustration, injury or accidents affecting head sometimes.

Health for Life Code #7

Your Heart, Mind, and your emotions are weakened when your blood is impure. Diseases include diabetes, drug addiction, alcohol, smoking, heart problems, depression, and Skin problems

Health for Life Code #8

Your Bowels, your body shape and your chakras are in danger from illness. Diseases include constipation, back pain, obesity, twisted uterus, tumors and foot pains

Health for Life Code #9

All of your body is weak, especially your blood system. Water is important. Diseases include high blood pressure, diabetes, cancer, accidents, and injury in fights, drowning, alcoholism and smoking.

The health of cats, dogs and any animal can be ascertained also if their birth date or *life code* is known. The above characteristics will also apply to the animals similarly. Machinery, cars as well as any type of vehicle are also determined health wise depending on their date of origin or the year they were built.

CHAPTER 8

Equation #7 – The Child Sequence Code

THE POSITION OF THE CHILD IN THE LINE OF CHILDREN BORN DETERMINES THE CHILD SEQUENCE CODE.
(Abortions are not counted, only all those alive)
The 1ˢᵗ child is considered to be Child Sequence code #1 and so on.

A system is as powerful as its constituents, and the sequence number determines the strength of each constituent. In human families the number of children has a lot to do with how each child will experience his or her life. It also will determine who will be weakest or strongest in health, wealth, happiness, love life, children joy and more. Let's take a look at the effects on a live of each number child from 1 to 9 of the life reality codes.

Life Code #1

Health will be affected if your are the first child

Life Code #2

Happiness and love will grace your life.

Life Code #3

Children or lack of children will affect your life

Life Code #4

You will work very hard in your life for low pay

Life Code #5

You will travel, be happy and move to many places

Life Code #6

You will experience family troubles and separations

Life Code #7

You will have love & communication problems, addiction

Life Code #8

Money and good looking people in your life, Prosperity

Life Code #9

You will struggle for money, and be suspicious of everyone

The above sequence interpretations can also be applied to houses, products, and inanimate system orders as well as animate. For example the 6th house in a block will experience possible robbery or fire or divorces but the 2nd house in the block may never experience those factors. You will find also that the 1st house in the block always consist of some one who spends a lot of time alone or the person is one who has to do everything by themselves.

With regard to the children sequence in a family if the number 1 dies, then you must remember the *equation changes in the family* as well as the sequence. In this case the 2nd child now becomes the first child and then the 3rd child now becomes the 2nd so the whole foundation of that person's life now gets adjusted. Of course this happens no matter where that child lives. **Twins are counted as one.** If the twins come after the 3rd child for example then both of the twins are counted as one. Usually the 1st of the twins will die first 95% of the time, as has been observed.

Anyway as the sequences changes then the 6th child who may have been sick will now recover from that illness, since the new sequence for that person will now become the 5th child which is a happier sequence code number. However take notice also that the 7th child will become the 6th child so he or she will now have difficult time in life. So as you can see, death of family members do affect the rest of the family, contrary to what people may think.

Remember The Apollo Moon landing rockets. Apollo 11 and 12 were very successful, Apollo 13 had to turn back and Apollo 15 had trouble. The sequence number of each product produced by a production system is very important in Vedic Mathematics. An interesting research on this subject would be to examine the fact that every 6th or 9th car produced by the Automobile manufacture will have troubles.

CHAPTER 9

Equation #8 – The Sexual Code

THE SEXUAL CODE IS THE SAME AS YOUR LIFECODE

Human sexuality is foremost in a relationship. In the following paragraphs you will find out what are your likes and dislikes in your sexuality or that of your partner's. By knowing this quality about your partner it is hoped that you will understand why they react to you they do because of their sexual secrets or experience in life. You can determine your sexual nature by reading the paragraph under your *life code* number.

Sexual Code #1

Male

Likes to be the Dominant one. He does not like to have an aggressive lover or partner. He wants to be the one to initiate lovemaking first. Most have had an early experience or abuse with sexuality.

Female

Likes to be surprised by her lover. Worries when her lover does not make love to her. Almost all females experience sexual abuse when young. Sometimes too self centered and too independent-may become lonely. Her obsession with her lover can lead to Cruelty & revenge when rejected.

Sexual Code #2

Male

Can make love many times per day if allowed. Has a greater appetite for sex than most men. Loves to look at women, and thinks all are pretty. Usually they can become gay if abused early in life.

Has to be careful what they say to their lovers. Likes to eat sweets-it actually helps him enjoy sex more if skinny.

Female

Is always ready for love at any time she is ready. Would fall asleep quickly after love making. Likes to be pampered in bed and embraced when making love. Must be hugged tightly if a good experience with orgasm is required. Likes to eat sweets-it actually helps them enjoy sex more. Has to be careful what they say to their lovers.

Sexual Code #3

Male

Can experience soft erections or premature ejaculation. Has a strong ego and does not care whether partner experience orgasms or not. Tend to get excited quickly and may not spend time on foreplay. Has a strong need for sex when eating properly and not unhealthy. Usually very skinny people but when overweight will suffer from premature ejaculation.

Female

Can experience Uterus & menstrual problems in life that will affect their love life. They love to have sex all the time, but cannot because of ego problems. Like to hear sex talk on phone or in bed before lovemaking. Likes to be talked dirty to when making love and also to experience a great orgasm. Usually very skinny people but when overweight will suffer from lack of desire for sex

Sexual Code #4

Male

Very strong and stable sex life if not working too hard. Stress is his biggest problem in their sex life - it hurts. Will despise sex after a while if they were abused early. Can suffer from Diabetes and High Blood pressure problems. Usually are very strong sexual partners and good lovers.

Female

Very strong and stable sex life if not working too hard. Stress is their biggest problem in their sex life - it hurts. Will despise sex after a while if they were abused early. Women here are too direct in their criticism - bad for the men. Can be very cold with their lover and husbands - too cold sometimes. Women tend to suffer from Sexual frigidity or painful love making. When attached to her lover will demand constant attention

Sexual Code #5

Male

Strong sexuality and good lovers when it comes to sex. Likes to be the dominant partner in this area of life. In some cases willing to do it only when he or she is ready, and does not care about the feelings of the partner. Likes to fantasize and to have more than one lover.

Female

Strong sexuality and good lovers when it comes to sex. Likes to be the dominant partner in this area of life. In some cases will want o do it only when they are ready, and does not care about the feelings of the partner. Many women suffer from a twisted womb and uterus problems. Could experience childhood sexual abuse, causing bad sexual fears. Sometimes they are beautiful women within a man's mind.

Sexual Code #6

Male

Strong and passionate lovers, but very dominant. Will take advantage of opposite sex using their power. Usually experience some kind of disappointment in love early in their life which makes them happy lover later in life.

Female

Strong and passionate lovers, but very dominant. Can suffer from severe Uterus or womb problems in life. Could end up removing the Uterus by surgery in older years. Will suffer from excessive menstrual bleeding and cramps. May experience abortions and miscarriages if eating too much meat.

Sexual Code #7

Male

Secret and quiet lovers who are wild when in the bedroom. Appears quiet but is a tiger when it comes to love making. Can have many secret lovers but few people will know of them. Will not hesitate to use drugs, alcohol and other stimulants to achieve desires. Can suffer from impotence if eating habits are not properly monitored.

Female

Secret and quiet lovers who are wild when in the bedroom. Appears quiet but is a tiger when it comes to love making. Can have many secret lovers but few people will know of them. Can suffer from Diabetes and loss of desire if diet is bad many women in this code may become strippers and Barmaids or bartenders, or erotic dancers on stage

Sexual Code #8

Male

Likes women and would like to make love to all of them. Admires beautiful women and likes to wine & dine them. Has a taste for expensive and extravagant life styles. Will have many lovers and may even do it for money. Dresses very expensively and neatly and are very good looking. Loves to do their own business and will be good in sales.

Female

Will suffer from Constipation and Lower Pelvic problems. May experience coldness and frigidity in love life. Will have many lovers and will even do it for money. Many women will become actresses and models .Will not hesitate to perform sex for promoting her life. Dresses very expensively and neatly and are very good looking and beautiful. Likes to go out on the town for fun - hates staying home. Loves to do their own business and will be good in sales. He or she can become selfish & stupid because of her beauty. Can be self centered so much that he or she never gets married. Will definitely become a revengeful lover if ever hurt by lover

Sexual Code #9

Male

Loves to have sex and will have a lot of energy for it. They are very emotional in their love making and like to please their partners. They have a lot of energy and are usually always ready for their partner. After marriage they become dull and scarce in their lovemaking, and may not do it for months.

Female

Has a perfect and sexually attractive body most times. Will love to have sex with strong men. Hates a weak man. Likes to be conquered and will usually let loose in their love making. The appetite is insatiable sometimes, and they think they never get enough. Gets confused with having many lovers. Loves to curl themselves like a snake around the man. Tend to become tense and quarrelsome when they do not get enough sex in their lives.

CHAPTER 10

Equation #9 – The Location Code

**THE LOCATION CODE IS DETERMINED BY
THE NUMBER LOCATION OF THE ADDRESS**
for example if the address is 122-34 56 street, only the 122-34 is
counted

Add up the digits of the building or home number to get a single digit as the Building Code. For example, if your house address is 3149 Macabee Drive, add the 3+1+4+9 and then reduce the results (17) to a single digit to get the Building Code, i.e. 1+7=8. The #8 is the Building Code for this address. The name of the street is not important. If the address were 3993, the Building Code would be #6. Now add up your address number on your home (or apartment) and then read the interpretation of your house code below.

The Location Code #1

This home is usually a very large home or in the extreme very small. People who live in this home are achievers and individualistic personalities who are constantly seeking to lead and dominate. This indicates that new ideas are created or new projects are being thought of constantly in this home.

People who are negative in this type of home are usually lonely and tend to seek solitary moments when they are troubled. To avoid any and all troubles, they should welcome all visitors in this home as special guests and always give them something to drink or something to eat. Divine pictures must be placed in the eastern corner of the house.

The Location Code #2

A loving couple sometimes resides in this home. Individuals living here are very cooperative and helpful to each other and to visitors. True love between the residents of this home exists and children are also well behaved in the home. Usually this home is a medium-sized home and is well decorated by the elder females in the house. Food is cooked always in this home and the inhabitants love to shop and decorate.

To obtain maximum benefits in this location one should be very cooperative, generous and kind to all. A picture of mother or grandmothers should be maintained in the northern corner of this house and, for Christians, a picture of the Virgin Mary should be maintained in the same location.

The Location Code #3

A home with this number consists of all comforts, lots of food and a lot to drink. Some of these homes are extremely large also. A large television or movie rack is definitely a part of this home. The occupants of this home are very youthful looking and there are usually many children living in this home. The absence of children in this home will indicate that unhappiness exists here. A library is also present and people in this home are supposed to read a lot of books.

In this home also many people find it very comfortable to pursue educational studies and the children who live here will definitely attend some college or university. Little angels or child angels govern this house. Pictures of child angels should be kept in the eastern corner of the house. A sacred heart picture of Christ should be maintained in the same corner for getting rid of negative forces in this home.

The Location Code #4

This is an extremely large home. Usually these buildings are divided into several units. Sometimes part of it is rented. It is a home that requires constant maintenance and work. People living in these homes are always trying to build their lives upward, and the women of the home are constantly complaining that their domestic work is never finished. There is always a presence of religious statues and pictures in this home. The individuals living in this home work very hard for very low income. However, their life takes an upward trend very slowly and surely. A picture of Buddha or Christ in a meditative posture should be maintained to avoid quarrels in the home between couples.

The Location Code #5

Sex, romance and love are very prevalent in this home. The negative qualities to look out for here are deceit, fraud, and false hopes. Women in this come are usually very attractive in appearance. People in this home also who are spiritual are constantly traveling. Almost everyone in this home owns a car and in some cases one person may own two cars. The couple who lives here is also very loving and the women are extremely beautiful looking. The men in this home are usually not fat. This home can also be a very lucky one for conducting business or professional services. There are also very high negative forces that can affect the individual in this home if they are not spiritual. Usually these homes have many cars or are surrounded by cars. People living in this home should avoid having illicit affairs or lustful thinking. A picture of Solomon or the angel Gabriel should be maintained in the eastern corner.

The Location Code #6

Disagreements, quarrels, tension and responsibilities are the effects felt in this home. People living here who are lazy or irresponsible will suffer extremely hard emotional feelings in this home. Negative people will end up quarrelling with each other. Husband and wife will sleep separately from each other. Financial problems could become a reality if red meat is maintained as a regular part of the diet. Health can also be affected and if the payments for mortgage are not maintained, the residents of this home could end up in foreclosure. To avoid all these negatives constant meditation should be maintained. A special room should be dedicated to the Lord, as this house is an extremely large one. Tempers should be controlled. Duty should be the priority of all the residents in this home and a picture of John the Baptist should be maintained in a Christian home.

The Location Code #7

This is a very large home also. A religious person or persons live in this home. The residents here are very slow in their actions and very laid back in their lifestyle. If a negatively rich individual owns this home, drugs, alcohol, and other addictions become prevalent here. Many of the activities in this home can be very secretive and the residents are constantly thinking or worrying about something. A positive effect on the house is that the residents here sleep very well and usually the beds are very large. Religious persons living here are usually very peaceful and are protected by divine forces. People in these homes should avoid criticizing and gossiping about others. Also, a picture of the cross without Christ should be maintained in the eastern corner of the home. A picture of Christ on the cross should be maintained in north side of this home.

The Location Code #8

This is an extravagant, luxurious and large home. This can be an apartment building, a duplex or a home with several floors. The individuals in this home are extremely rich. Their income is high. Their furniture is expensive and their bills are high. Money comes very easily to the residents of this home and if negative, expenses will come instead. If the residents of this home are negative or have been cruel to others, eventually they are struck with serious sickness or diseases as a result of karma. For good luck the individuals should avoid excessive gambling or drinking or waste. For religious individuals, a picture of the brilliant Sun should be maintained in the eastern corner of the house. A picture of full moon should be maintained in the same position. People in the house are involved in some kind of business or investment.

The Location Code #9

This is usually a very large home, which is very expensive and which requires a lot of maintenance. If a negative person lives in this house, he or she will most likely suffer from an incurable disease. It is important that anyone living in this house should follow all religious rules of living and they should at all cost avoid eating red meat, drinking alcohol or taking drugs. It is also very important that an altar of God be maintained in this home so as to avoid all problems. People in these homes tend to become famous or well known in their community. Childbirth could be difficult during the months of pregnancy. Most of the individuals living in this home seek knowledge and other interests related to religion, astrology and philosophy. It is important that a picture or statue of all the angels and deities be maintained in this home in the eastern corner and Christians should have a shrine dedicated to the saints of the Old Testaments.

An Ideal Home for an Ideal Couple

Who is a gentleman? Any educated person may be a gentleman. But without having a legitimate wife, even an educated man cannot be gentleman. And after marriage, life cannot run without money. But no one gets money without efforts. Hence, marriage and taking up some economic occupation are necessary to be a civilized man. A civilized man must also make his residence at an excellent inhabitation, which is managed well. There must be water near the dwelling and the general environment must be as clean and pure as possible.

There must be two portions in a gentleman's house – one for storing necessary provisions and the other for sleeping. His bedroom must have a comfortable bedstead with soft cushions and white sheets. All the cosmetics must be handy in the bedroom. Apart from musical instruments, music system posters of natural scenes and love scenes of couples must decorate the bedroom.

The house must also have a swing, a lawn and a kitchen garden. The woman must use the inner portion of the house. It should have a bedstead with soft cushion. There must also be a smaller but comfortable bed nearby for lovemaking. The owner of the house must enjoy physical intimacy with his wife on this smaller bed. Light snacks and drinks must also be handy in this room. After a hard day's work, the evening of a gentleman must start with music. Guests may visit him at his time or the gentleman may visit someone else as a guest.

CHAPTER 11

Equation#10 – The Wealth Code

THE WEALTH CODE IS
THE SAME AS YOUR LIFE CODE#

Being wealthy means that you have gained a lot more than others. The first thing you have to remember is that "Nothing in this world is owned by you, the true owner is the universe", However when you own a piece of land, you own it mentally, because it still belongs to the Earth really. So also it is for everything else. Whatever we own we only own it while we possess it in our mind. So every asset or material wealth we own, we own it only on a Timeline. The only asset we own which goes with us when we die is knowledge and memories of our life. These are the only two types of wealth we own which cannot be inherited or sold by anyone else.

Every person looks at wealth differently. Some feel wealth is having love, some thinks that wealth is having a lot of money and others measure wealth by what they see others have. I think the greatest wealth is *Peace of mind*. The list below shows how each lifecode number thinks about wealth and how they view acquiring this wealth. Find your lifecode number then check the list below.

Life Code #1

Wealth is power to rule over others, worries about bills, seeks wealth as peace of mind

Life Code #2

Love and Romance is their greatest wealth. Views wealth as possession of people and material things

Life Code #3

Children is their greatest wealth, dreams of winning the lottery, gambles to get rich quick

Life Code #4

Work to get rich, will never get rich quick. Owning a home is their dream of wealth, good food and a good bed to rest.

Life Code #5

Business, Sales, and creating new products. Good marketers. Could try to get rich through deceiving other.

Life Code #6

Power, Politics, Police, Military are all the ways wealth will come. Could get rich thru lawsuits, courts and CEO jobs

Life Code #7

Astrology, Spirituality, Liquor stores, bars and clubs are all the ways he could get rich. Real estate is lucky for them

Life Code #8

Acting, Modeling, Movie making, Luxury businesses, jewelry and winning in investing and gambling will make you rich.

Life Code #9

Will have a hard time getting rich materially, but will be wealthy spiritually. Can get rich by criminal activities, which will be lost later. Will have hard time maintaining material wealth.

As you can see not all people are able to gather wealth easily. If a question was asked, 'What would you do with your life, if you had millions of dollars, and had no expenses'". The answer is that all that is left is good food, a loving spouse and children, a comfortable home to live in, and trips around the world. Ok, let's say you have all that, what next? The answer is, *"your legacy to the world"*. What will you do that people will remember you by? That is what makes live forever. That which money cannot buy, which is memories of you by as many people. The only price for this wealth is charity. You see this with Oprah Winfrey, Angelina Jolie, Donald Trump, Bill Gates and many others. From these people you can assess now that those who are rich and prosperous are those very people who become saints in the end. People who helps to promote life in the universe. Therefore we can conclude that when you give you will receive. Such is the equation of prosperity. Giving more to the universe makes it recognizes you as an expanding individual that benefits the future. So the universe in turn rewards you accordingly. Look at all the richest people in the world and you will see the equation of wealth. They give more than others to the world.

Oprah changed many people's lives and gave away a lot in charity. So has Donald Trump. Bill Gates changed the whole world with his computers and knowledge, and so on. They are not just lucky, they are angels who are here to bless us and give to the world.

Consider the reverse of this: OJ Simpson became wealthy; Nicole Simpson and others around him misused the money. You saw what happened if you followed the OJ Simpson case. Bernie Madoff was selfish and fraudulent and fell right down, taking with him all the selfish rich people who were wealthy and thought they owned part of the universe, forgetting that what they had was a gift from the universe. People forget that God owns everything and whatever you have is lent to you. It is taken away from you if you become selfish and ungrateful to the universe. Immortality is earned not given or transferred. Einstein, Newton, Christ, Gandhi, and Martin Luther King, Jr. and others did not have lots of money but they earned something money cannot buy…immortality.

CHAPTER 12

Equation #11 – The Prosperity Code

Let us look at how you can use your *life code* equation to determine what you should give in order to receive as well as when in your life you will have the opportunity to get rich. First of all here is a list of businesses according to your *Life Code* number that you should avoid if you wish to become rich and wealthy. Use firstly your lifecode to check the list below:

Life Code #1

Avoid partnerships, they will rob you.

Life Code #2

Avoid Business or sales, you are too generous

Life Code #3

Avoid get rich quick schemes, you will lose

Life Code #4

Avoid any business that involves traveling

Life Code #5

Avoid fraudulent or false schemes. Do not lie

Life Code #6

Avoid partnerships or businesses with family members

Life Code #7

Avoid involvement in Dark magic or secret schemes

Life Code #8

Avoid overspending, too much luxury & hasty investing

Life Code #9

Avoid trying to be too helpful by lending money or trust

A list of charities you should be involved in for the blessings of universal wealth…check it out according to your lifecode.
If your *life code* is…..

Life Code #1

Your charity should be with helping the Homeless

Life Code #2

Your charity should be with helping the Abused, Starving

Life Code #3

Your charity should be with helping the Children

Life Code #4

Your charity should be with helping the Hospitals

Life Code #5

Your charity should be with helping the counseling

Life Code #6

Your charity should be with helping the military

Life Code #7

Your charity should be with helping the temples

Life Code #8

Your charity should be with helping the farmers

Life Code #9

Your charity should be with helping the Homeless, helping poor people, charity.

ADD YOUR LIFECODE # TO THE NUMBER 8 TO FIND YOUR PROSPERITY CODE e.g. Lifecode #3 + 8 = 12 → 1+2 =3 = Prosperity Code

Now check the list below for your PROSPERITY CODE interpretation

Prosperity Code #1

You will enjoy great wealth and comfort, and will be owner of many assets etc.

Prosperity Code #2

You will gain lots of wealth after marriage and thru your partner and friends

Prosperity Code #3

After Education and knowledge comfort comes -but will get wealthy thru children

Prosperity Code #4

Only hard work and dedication will sustain you. Income & expenses will be even

Prosperity Code #5

Your fortune will come from a far, Avoid partnerships, income will be up & down

Prosperity Code #6

Fortunes will come from family and inheritance. Can lose wealth through Ego etc.

Prosperity Code #7

If not secretive, Wealth will be lost. Love brings wealth, Greed destroys wealth

Prosperity Code #8

Will always have money but must control spending. Large gains, Big losses, Ego

Prosperity Code #9

Will struggle for wealth, Will not win lottery. Must be creative to gain wealth

CHAPTER 13

Equation #12 – The Name Sound Code

THE NAME SOUND CODE IS THE CODE OF THE FIRST VOWEL IN YOUR NAME. In the English language there are only 5 vowels, A, E, I O, U that are called vocals or independent vibrations, without these vocals, words cannot be formed)

Vocals can be positive or negative. If a name begins with a negative sound then any element that is given that name will experience the quality of that name. The various sounds in the universe are made up of 9 different vibrations just as we have 9 different electromagnetic energies in Sunlight. We can represent these main sounds by using what we call "vowels" in our language and auditory system. They are as follows:

A, AA, AAH .... = 1 – Powerfully independent, Creative

E, EE, IE.......... = 5 – Like money, expensive things, good looking

I, AY, UY.......... = 9 – Struggle, Confused, conflicting, worried

O, OH, AU......... = 7 – Secretive, emotional, not expressive, ego

U, OO, HU......... = 6 – Power hungry, strong ego, suspicious, pain

You will notice that the names that begin with the letter "I" or one that carries the sound UY or AY, are names that struggle to expand or progress. For example countries with names starting with letter "I" such as Israel, Iraq, India, and Iran are all countries that are conflicting, confused and unable to make progress without struggles. Notice that countries such as Syria, Lebanon, Egypt are all countries without the "I" sound in the beginning. They are not so conflicted and are less controversial.

Look at names of people you know, you will find their personality and characteristics match their first name sound. You will find that this science of naming of something applies powerfully in the naming of a child. If the child is named with an "I" sound then that child will struggle much in his or her childhood. The ancient Indian sages prohibited naming a child unless the wise men were consulted. Usually when a child is named with the first sound or vowel " I ", some one old could die in the family soon after the child is born.

This equation also applies to other things like streets, villages, towns, and more. Among the batteries made "Duracell" batteries are the most expensive and longer lasting than other batteries, Notice the "Ü' for power. The company IBM suffered lots of setbacks in business. Business names are important. If the business name first vibration is an "I" or an O, it will fail in the beginning. Hollywood movie "Nine" failed many times before its completion. The movie ET was a success, and so on.

In the name or identity of anything, the name must contain a vowel followed by a consonant sound or the vowel sound is preceded by a consonant. Sounds and words are formed by bringing consonants and vowels together. There are infinite numbers of auditory variations of sounds that can be formed in the universe. There are only 9 colors of basic light forms but only a limited amount of color variations can be formed compared to the unlimited variety of sound formations in the universe. This is why music can affect our innermost being, our thoughts and our soul, which is beyond the physical body. These vibrations become part of our life. If your name was LUANA for example, as your life progresses and as you grow the sound of your name become attached to you more and more until it becomes your complete shadow or soul within you. It is one of the most recognized intangible identification of your self. The letters in your name forms also a time line equation in your life in the form of a wave vibration. Each letter has a positive or negative or neutral vibration. Here are the vibrations attached to each letter of the English alphabet.

A = NEUTRAL	B = POSITIVE
C = POSITIVE	D = NEUTRAL
E = POSITIVE	F = NEGATIVE
G = NEUTRAL	H = POSITIVE
I = NEGATIVE	J = NEUTRAL

K = POSITIVE	L = POSITIVE
M = NEUTRAL	N = POSITIVE
O = NEUTRAL	P = POSITIVE
Q = NEGATIVE	R = NEGATIVE
S = POSITIVE	T = NEUTRAL
U = POSITIVE	V = NEGATIVE
W = NEUTRAL	X = POSITIVE
Y = NEUTRAL	Z = POSITIVE

If your name was LUCAS for example you can find out the sum vibration of your life by finding out how many negatives and positives in your life. In this case

L = POSITIVE   a positive sine wave value
U = POSITIVE   a positive sine wave value
C = POSITIVE   a positive sine wave value
A = NEUTRAL   a neutral sine wave value
S = POSITIVE   a positive sine wave value

Four positives and one neutral indicate a somewhat successful life. Now try that with your name and see the results.

CHAPTER 14

Equation #13 – The Name Cycle

THE NAME CYCLE CODE IS DETERMINED BY THE POSITION OF THE LETTERS IN YOUR NAME AND IS COMPARED TO YOUR AGE BY MATCHING EACH LETTER WITH 9 YEARS OF YOUR LIFE STARTING WITH THE 1ST LETTER AND AGE 0

Using the letters of your name you can also do a timeline of your life. In the Vedic Science of reality, each letter represents 9 years of your life. So the first letter in your name will represent 0 to 9 and the 2nd letter will represent 9 to 18 and so on. If you look at the name Lucas above it will indicate most of Lucas's life up to age 45 is mostly positive. He will still experience some learning hurdles in the process but he will learn most of his lessons in the neutral and negative periods in his life when he will meet most of the tests in his life   each letter forms a vibration that places us in a cycle that teaches us lessons of life. When your parents give you this name you have, they must think carefully about what they want their child to experience. Of course the letters in your name also reflects what the mother and father was experiencing during the gestation period of the pregnancy, so the vibration of your name which comes from the mouth of your parents carries with it all the karmas experienced in those 9 months.

Add 9 years to each letter of your name in the following equation and find out how you will progress in your life during those cycles. Key words are given below to help you understand the vibration effects of the letters in your name. It's a work table to write in you letter and your age.

1. 1st letter......_____   = Age 0 to 9   _____
2. 2nd letter......_____   = Age 9 to 18   _____
3. 3rd letter......_____   = Age 18 to 27   _____
4. 4th letter......_____   = Age 27 to 36   _____

5. 5th letter......_____ = Age 36 to 45 _____
6. 6th letter......_____ = Age 45 to 54 _____
7. 7th letter......_____ = Age 54 to 63 _____
8. 8th letter......_____ = Age 63 to 72 _____
9. 9th letter......_____ = Age 72 to 81 _____

Note: If your first and second names are less than nine letters, then you repeat your first name. For example, if your name is John Jay, which is 7 letters for cycles 1 through 7, for the 8th and 9th cycle, repeat the J and O from John (the first name).

Now here are the key words for each letter to place in the equation above so that you can know about your cycles

A = Independent   B = Romance & marriage
C = Comfort/children   D = High tempers/Low pay
E = prosperity   F = Responsibility/ Luxury
G = hard work   H = Business & gains
I = Struggles   J = Leadership/alone
K = Love/friendship   L = Happiness, Education
M = High stress   N = Travel and Moving
O = Life analysis/God   P = Investments/analysis
Q = Difficulties   R = Death /Fame/Spirits
S = Self-achievements   T = Career changes/Low pay
U = Power & Status   V = Winning, Frustration
W = Confused   X = Life changes, Deep studies
Y = Lonely & self   Z = Sexuality, Extravagance

Details of the name code numbers and additional details based on your name vibrations can be found in Swami Ram's book "The Vedic Name Code." Found at www.swamiram.com

The same table above can be used for check the vibration cycles of countries, products and more.

CHAPTER 15

Equation #14 – The Career Code

THE CAREER CODE IS THE SAME AS YOUR LIFECODE NUMBER AS WELL AS YOUR EDUCATIONAL CODE.

A wheel of a car fits exactly into the axle of the car. Here the wheel fulfills its function. When cooking the ingredients that you place into the pot determines the end success of the dish being prepared. Every ingredient was placed carefully as it's served its purpose for what it was made. Each of those ingredients had their own *life code* purpose. Sometimes you may find that a person you know hates mathematics in school while another may love it. Why do some people like reading, some like acting, and some like modeling while some cannot work with wood construction or metals. It's because we all are born with certain specific abilities and talents in life that will fulfill our purpose for living.

In this chapter we are going to look at several Equations of Life that enable us to calculate what kind of educational studies you should follow and also what kind of career you should follow that suits your karmic purpose here on earth. We will be able to identify the kind of great abilities you have and how you can use these to your advantage for maximum gain of happiness and satisfaction in life. First we will look at the Equations that affect you Educational abilities in the hope that you will know exactly what kind of courses you will perform best with in school. Using your basic lifecode we will calculate your CAREER CODE AND FIND YOUR CODE IN THE LIST BELOW:

Life Code #1

Your mind is fast and bright, but your independence does not allow you to be controlled by anyone. You like to take the lead in everything. You are creative so you love art, you will perform well in mathematics, engineering, graphic designs, and anything where you can use mental strength.

Life Code #2

Your mind is somewhat slower than others. You are not too fond of tedious calculations, so mathematical subjects will be difficult for you. You are decorative and helpful to all. You love music and will be attracted to food services. So singing, chefs, restaurant ownership, interior design, fashions, nursing, home care and other services are good for you. Take subjects that are related to these.

Life Code #3

You are very social. You like attention and want everyone to listen to you and you love children. Acting, Social services, Teaching, Dancing, marketing, beauty consultant, pediatrics, child care services and party planning are some of your talents. You should also study to work with the publishing industry and Computer sciences

Life Code #4

You are very strong headed, hard working and dedicated to your work. You make wonderful students and employees. Manufacturing, civil engineering, industrial sciences, accounting, farming, real estate, building construction and masonry are some of the career you can follow. Take subjects related to these. You also make good doctors and lab technicians.

Life Code #5

You are a busy body. You cannot sit one place, you like to keep moving. You get bored easily so you need a career that keeps changing like the internet. Travel industry, Airlines, Counselors in marriage and love, consultants, lecturers, Automobile industry, Moving businesses, Modeling Computer sciences, electronics and scientific research.

Life Code #6

You get frustrated easily, you like to argue and you love power. You are a true attorney and politician at heart. You love to be in the limelight. You never want to think you are wrong, and will oppose anyone who comes against you. You love to correct others. Government positions, leadership positions, medical doctors, mechanical engineers, military, police, Teaching, Exercise instructor, Industrial designs, architect, Real estate, Mortgages, credit services, and management are some of the subjects your should study.

Life Code #7

You keep thoughts to yourself, you are religious, you are emotional and you always consider other people's feeling. Your mind is constantly analyzing and thinking. Because of this you can become a great priest. Many people in your lifecode become bar owners, Club owners. This may affect your love life negatively. Good careers are computer sciences, chemists, biologists, Medicine, Magicians, pharmacy, Nurses, Home care, Analysts, consultants and secret agents.

Life Code #8

You are extravagant; you love luxury, money, comfort and higher class level of society. You can dress well, speak well and love to act. You make a great salesperson. Since you know how to make deals, business, investing or owning a store will be profitably. Fashion designing, acting, architectural design, and sales are your talents

Life Code #9

You love water, likes to take long showers and spend time at the beach. Shipping, Sea work, government employees, Court careers such as lawyers, judges, bailiffs etc. are good for you. You also make good politicians, advisors, teachers, congressmen (women), Gurus, writers and Lifeguards. Because you get confused in your life easily about your goals and objectives, you should take courses that are more challenging to your personality that keeps you busy.

FIND THE BEST JOBS FOR YOU BY CAREER CODES

LIFE CODE #1

Attorney, computer, detective, hospital, jewelers, medical field, photography, priests, prison, programmers, teacher, astrologer, sheriff, barber, police, surgeon, inspector, judge, physician, magistrate, principal, dentist, mines, coal, navy, guru, yoga, minister, well digger, lawyer, poet.

LIFE CODE #2

Butcher, city, fashion, lottery, military, retail stores, sales, state, use of weapons, mineral, merchant, gambler, trading, captain, officer, broker.

LIFE CODE #3

Airlines, alcohol/drugs, astrology, automobile, computers, detectives, hospitals, jeweler, medical field, photography, priest, programmers, transportation, astrologer, interpretation, dancer, surgeon, mathematician, physician, dentist, mines, navy, tailor, car salesman, chemist, poet.

LIFE CODE #4

Accounting, agriculture, banking, butchers, city, construction, courts, farming, government, insurance, IRS, military, real estate, state, stock, exchange, mechanic, use of weapons, metals, potter, factory, engineer, bank agent, geology, steam, engines, engineering, captain, contractor, officer, bank clerk, technician.

LIFE CODE #5

Airlines, amusements, artist, automobile, communication, journalist, printing, publishing, transportation, interpretation, cloths sales, athlete, cowherd, dancer, mathematician, textiles, paper press, tailor, car, salesman, chemist, writer, literature, stenographer, cineactor.

LIFE CODE #6

Accounting, agriculture, banking, construction, courts, farming, food services, government, insurance, IRS, music, real state, restaurant, stock exchange, mechanic, metal, musician, potter, cook factory, engineer, bank agent, geology, steam engines, literature, stenographer, cineactor.

LIFE CODE #7

Amusements, artist, communication, electrical, journalist, management, printing, publishing, sculptor, expert, clothes, sales, athlete, cowherd, leader, textiles, paper press, writer, literature, stenographer, cineactor.

LIFE CODE #8

Attorney, food service, music, politics, prison, restaurant, teacher, sheriff, musician, barber, cook, police, inspector, judge, magistrate, principal, coal, guru, yoga minister, well digger, lawyer, criminal.

LIFE CODE #9

Electrical, fashion, lottery, management, retail stores, sales, sculptor, expert, minerals, merchant, gambler, leader, trading, writer, artist, and broker.

A person who does not seek knowledge and education for his own benefit will never be able to find his or her life's purpose. All people are encouraged to seek a Guru or advisor in life. Your relationship with your teacher is very important. Only a good advisor can lead you to a good path in life. We are all at the mercy of our guides and gurus. A bad guru or teacher will bring your life downward; a good one will make you prosperous. Our first teachers are our parents. Later in this book we will be looking at relationships and you will be able to determine your relationship with your Guru or teacher or advisor.

The address location of the school you attend, the address location of the place you work at, are all important to the success of your life purpose on Earth. Later, we will take a look at how all these equations play a great part in making your life a success or failure. The Location codes are important for your life success

CHAPTER 16

Equation # 15 – The Investment Code

THE INVESTMENT CODE IS THE LIFECODE # PLUS THE CODE OF YOUR INVESTMENT CATEGORY CODE

When people invest in a home – the American dream – the stock market or in a business of their own, and then surprisingly lose it in a few months or a few years, they and their friends often wonder what caused such a loss. Most of the time it is due to lack of knowledge of business strategies or the timing of when the investment was made.

What you need to know now is whether you will be successful in any particular type of investments and what investments are good for you. When you invest in a certain type of investment, your chances of gaining a profit may be greater than in certain other types. The most important factors that govern any investment are type, timing and matching with karmic Codes of Life. As Shakespeare said: "Some are born great. Some achieve greatness. And some have greatness thrust upon them."

Not everyone is suitable for certain types of investments; so knowing what types of investments are suitable for you increases your chances of making profits and becoming wealthy. On the Table 27.1, I have selected the most popular types of investments that can be compared to your Life Code to help you understand the best types of investments that you can get into. However, it doesn't mean you should shut out other investments completely. Perhaps a partner, who is compatible with you, would be able to work with certain investments that are negative with your *Life code* but positive with your partner's Life code.

In the following table you will find a selected set of investment categories that can be matched against your *Life Code*. The result is your Investment Code

INVESTMENT CATEGORY CODES

- ❖ REAL ESTATE AND LAND   = 4
- ❖ STOCK MARKET   = 4
- ❖ CONSULTANTS   = 5
- ❖ COURT AND POLICE   = 6
- ❖ COSMETICS AND BEAUTY SALON   = 8
- ❖ HOSPITALS & MEDICAL   = 7
- ❖ MORTGAGES & BANKS   = 4
- ❖ FARMING AND AGRICULTURE   = 4
- ❖ SHIPPING AND BOATS   = 9
- ❖ SHOPS AND STORES   = 8
- ❖ RESTAURANTS AND FOOD CATERERS   = 2
- ❖ MANUFACTURING AND BUILDING   = 4
- ❖ PUBLISHING & PRINTING   = 3
- ❖ MODELLING AND FASHIONS   = 8
- ❖ YOGA AND MEDITATION   = 3
- ❖ COMPUTERS AND TECHNOLOGY   = 7

Check the Investment Category Code then add it to your Lifecode number, Use the result to read below the Investment Code that matches your life in that category.

Investment Code #1

- You have to do it all by yourself – having a partner is trouble.
- To make this investment profitable you need to maintain and research all information about it.
- Try to seek leadership and creativity in this investment, as this helps you improve profits.
- Avoid becoming too dominant.

Investment Code #2

- A good business doing partner ship with spouse, friend or family member

- You always make profits as long as your relationship with the people involved is positive.
- Learn to be very cooperative with the people you meet in this investment and watch what you say, as this can cause you losses.

Investment Code #3

- Many opportunities present themselves in this business for you.
- Always maintain constant knowledge about your investments, and then your profits will always be high.
- Try to maintain a good sense of humor as it brings profits.
- Avoid childishness or immature controlling of others.

Investment Code #4

- This investment requires that you work very hard.
- No matter how hard you work, you have to work harder to make any profits with this investment.

Investment Code #5

- A constant changing investment, which requires rapid thinking and action before you can become successful.
- Constant change and new ideas are needed to make this investment profitable.
- Watch out for fraudulent and deceptive people.

Investment Code #6

- An investment that requires research, responsibility and power.
- This investment should never have a partnership.
- Avoid confrontation, conflicts and disagreements in this investment as you may lose your investment.
- Watch out for thieves and robbers.

Investment Code #7

- This investment must be done with the utmost discretion and secrecy.

- All transactions in this investment should be done with caution, and profits will come to you slowly but surely.
- Research into the background of this investment, as there may be secret pitfalls awaiting you.

Investment Code #8

- A very lucrative and profitable investment.
- Invest as much as you can and with good timing your sales will become profitable.
- Most of the people you contact regarding this investment will want to be paid their fair share.

Investment Code #9

- You should avoid this type of investment.
- Extreme caution is needed with his investment or else you will lose a great deal of money.
- Try to invest as little as you can and do not spend too much money on improvements, as this will create very little profit.
- Buying and selling quickly is better as a sort term investment.
- Consult with a priest regarding your investment.

CHAPTER 17

Equation # 16 – The Vehicle Code

THE VEHICLE CODE APPLIES TO ALL TYPES OF VEHICLES AND IS OBTAINED BY ADDING UP THE DIGITS OF THE YEAR THE VEHICLE IS MADE for example if the year of the car or truck is 2005 the Vehicle Code is 7 (2+0+0+5)

The human body is a vehicle itself. It carries with it all the parts of the human body. A car can be compared to the human body the same way. It has a circulatory system, a brain, and eyes, which are the headlights. The horn is like the mouth; its fuel is like its stomach; and its wheels are its feet, and so on. You get the point! Therefore we should treat the car or vehicle as if it's another person or entity fetching us around in its belly.

You will find that if you add up the digits in the year of the cars or the vehicle you will find that you will be able to determine what type of breakdowns and repairs, the vehicle will experience. For example if your take the year 1998 and add the digits 1 +9+ 9+ 8 = 27 which is also equal to the final number 9. You will find that these cars will experience lots of breakdowns and accidents which total the vehicle but will rarely harm its occupants in an accident. If year of the car or vehicle number adds up to a final digit of 6, such as the year 2004, you will find that those cars will be trouble some and may experience fatal accidents. Drivers cars made in these years are asked to be cautious. The following table indicates the effects of your car or vehicle according to the year it was produced or manufactured. You must first add up the digits in the year to get the final number. This will apply to any type of moving vehicle or machinery. For example a 2009 car is a car with a lifecode #2 (2 +0+0+9 = 11=> 1+1=2). Now check your car and its spiritual qualities in the list below.

Each car or vehicle has a *Life Code*, which in Vedic Science is known as the Vehicle Code. This code identifies the vehicle by its year of origin and describes all the possible problems than can affect the car and gives the inner and outer strength of the vehicle itself.

Now check your car or vehicle codes below:

Vehicle Code #1 – All about your Car, Truck or Vehicle's condition

- Good car, that will prove reliable
- Driving alone most of the time
- Problem starting sometimes or with lights and ignition area
- Usually has books and signs inside or outside the vehicle
- Listens to talk shows while you drive.

Vehicle Code #2 – All about your Car, Truck or Vehicle's condition

- This car will transport many people and will be used for shopping.
- Always have music playing while you drive.
- Romance, love and sex will be influenced by this car.
- The driver will always have company while driving.
- Problems in this car will be with seats, crowded trunk and problems with the inside of the car.
- Front end problems

Vehicle Code #3 – All about your Car, Truck or Vehicle's condition

- Children will be part of this car's transport
- This car will have an elaborate musical and speaker system
- Most problems will be with the steering and guidance system.

Vehicle Code #4 – All about your Car, Truck or Vehicle's condition

- This car will be used primarily for job or career services.
- A solid car and it could experience manufacturing problems.
- The engine is stronger than the body of the car.

Vehicle Code #5 – All about your Car, Truck or Vehicle's condition

- This car accumulates a lot of mileage.
- This car has wheel or transmission problems.
- This car will change many hands quickly.
- Usually a sports car, a race car or fast car.

Vehicle Code #6 – All about your Car, Truck or Vehicle's condition

- Lots of repairs and possible accident with this car.
- Lots of traffic tickets.

- You may experience loan payment problems with this car.
- This car may have had an accident before you owned it and may be accident-prone.
- Owner will spend lots of money on body repairs or exhaust system.

Vehicle Code #7 – All about your Car, Truck or Vehicle's condition

- There will be oil or water problems.
- This car will be used for religious purposes.
- The owners are usually religious.
- The driver will experience much thinking while driving
- The atmosphere inside of the car will always be quiet
- If a negative person owns this car, he will be smoking or drinking alcohol or be addicted to something.
- Problems with this car may involve the controlling components of the engine.

Vehicle Code #8 – All about your Car, Truck or Vehicle's condition

- A luxurious and expensive car.
- Most of these cars are custom made and rare.
- The driver experiences much comfort and may even have a chauffeur.
- The driver may also be a designer or model or actor in film or a businessman.

Vehicle Code #9 – All about your Car, Truck or Vehicle's condition

- Water problems and possible radiator problems.
- Usually the first thing to go is the water pump or the fuel pump.
- Possible accident will damage the car but little injury to the driver.
- Owner will spend lots of money on repairs and maintenance.

CHAPTER 18

Equation #17 – The Vehicle Comfort code

THE VEHICLE COMFORT CODE DETERMINES HOW YOU ENJOY YOUR VEHICLE AND IS OBTAINED BY ADDING YOUR LIFECODE # TO THE VEHICLE CODE OF THE VEHICLE for e.g. if your lifecode is #5 and the car vehicle code is 9 the it is 9 +5 = 14 →1 +4 = 5 = your Vehicle Comfort Code

The human body is made to walk on Earth. When it is elevated off the Earth in a vehicle such as a plane, it must respond to the movements of that vehicle. The vehicle of course would respond with its own energy field together with the energy field of the human person. A measure of the resulted energy field would most likely tell how that car or vehicle would respond to your energy field when you are in it.

The Vehicle Comfort Code #1

- Problems with accepting the car
- You will spend a lot of time driving this car alone.
- This car will hardly be driven on the road.
- You will worry about the payments on this car.
- All responsibility of car will fall on the owner.

The Vehicle Comfort Code #2

- A very comfortable car.
- Lots of shopping by the owner of this car.
- The car will be well decorated inside.
- Lots of music will be played in this car.
- Someone will always be transported in this car.

The Vehicle Comfort Code #3

- A party car that never misses a party.
- A very comfortable car that will be popular.
- Will experience problems with children in this car.

- A skinny person will drive this car a lot.
- Lots of books or papers in this car.
- A phone or TV system will be in this car.

The Vehicle Comfort Code #4

- A car that is solid and reliable
- This car can have body problems later.
- You will be very stressed out
- Car will mostly be used for going to work
- Hard to find the destination

The Vehicle Comfort Code #5

- You will drive this vehicle a great deal.
- Your car may be used for long distance travel.
- The owners of this car will enjoy romance and love.
- Air filters should be changed very often on this car.
- Problems with this car may involve the wheels, alignment or break repairs maybe required often.

The Vehicle Comfort Code #6

- Problems with this car may involve accidents, traffic tickets and collision.
- Make sure you have good insurance coverage and follow all rules.
- The body of this car may experience scratches or dents.
- Make sure you do regular tune-ups and maintenance as needed.
- Police will notice you very often while driving this car.
- You will have a high credit debt on or high payments.
- If you lease, it's better than buying outright.

The Vehicle Comfort Code #7

- A very quiet, comfortable and smooth driving with this car
- You will constantly be in deep thought while driving this car
- There may be religious pictures and air fresheners in this car

- A good car for you to take on a long drive.
- The only problems for this car will be the inside engine parts and the liquids such as the coolants, etc.

The Vehicle Comfort Code #8

- This car will be an expensive or luxury car fully loaded
- This car could be a limousine, town car or luxury sedan
- The price of this car will be high and the car will be attractive
- The owner will be someone who makes a lot of money or he or she could very well be in business
- This car will be expensive to maintain and will involve love affairs with the opposite sex
- This may be a sports car or a race car

The Vehicle Comfort Code #9

- Be careful of accidents and breakdowns while driving
- Avoid driving too much if this is an old car
- You will experience traffic tickets and court problems while owning this car
- The cooling system and pumps are weak and will give problems
- Be prepared to spend lots of money on repairs etc.
- You could experience an accident that totals the car
- Make sure you ask a priest to bless the car before driving.

CHAPTER 19

Equation # 18 – The Money Code

THE MONEY CODE IS THE SAME AS YOUR LIFECODE

There is an old saying "Money grows on trees." You will be amazed that this old saying may be true after all. Only members of the plant kingdom provide foods to all animals and humans. Whatever we cook and eat is as a result of the growth of plants, trees and herbs. Whether it is the fruits from he trees, the roots or the leaves, they become our source of energy directly or indirectly. After eating our food, we obtain enough energy to work and earn money, which then we use to pay our bills and buy all things we desire. So it is safe to say that, "Money does come from trees."

Like all things, money should be respected and treated as a divine energy that is used by all of us to enjoy this world. There are nine forms of money energy, which affect all of us according to our actions in life. For example, you may notice that if we fail to perform our duties properly to our employers, we will be denied raises. Or another example is if we steal money from others, we will lose our wealth in many different ways.

Money Code #1

- You worry about money too much.
- Whenever you have too much money you feel you have power.
- Not having money makes you feel too dependent on others.
- Loss of money can cause you to be depressed.
- Avoid gambling, as you can become addicted to it.
- Too much greed for money can make you very abusive and very insulting.
- Think of your bills and pay them before pleasure.

Money Code #2

- You love to look for bargains and save money in shopping.
- You purchase items that are sometimes useless to you.
- Most of your money is spent on jewelry, clothes, and decorating the home.
- You have a secret stash of cash hidden away for hard times.
- Spending money on food or restaurants will be beneficial.
- You usually have money at all times.
- You like to spend your money to buy gifts for others.
- You cannot own your own business because you give away too much.

Money Code #3

- You dream of winning the lottery or jackpot; it could happen.
- You like to use money to buy toys and childish items.
- You use money as an opportunity to attract the attention of others.
- You may earn lots of money as teachers, actors and models.
- Money can create quarrels between you, your friends and lovers.
- Money used for books or readings will benefit you.

Money Code #4

- You have to work hard for your money.
- Most of your money coming in you will eventually spend out again.
- Sometimes you have to go through much sacrifice to make money.
- Lack of money causes you stress and depression.
- Avoid borrowing money, as it can be hard to pay back.
- Raises and promotions will be slow coming at work.
- Save as much as you can – bigger savings make you feel secure.

Money Code #5

- Money moves rapidly in your life.

- You'll make an excellent businessperson, as you're skilled in sales.
- Because of your skills with words, you can sell anything to anyone.
- A lot of your money is spent on cars, airlines, and traveling.
- You spend lots of money on pleasure and comfort.
- Females spend money mostly on fashion and gyms for exercise.
- You change your mind quickly when trying to purchase something for others.
- You may have problems with the revenue department – be honest with taxes.
- Avoid fraud, deception and robbery of others and money will love to be with you.

Money Code #6

- Lack of money makes you very frustrated and irresponsible.
- You must be careful, as credit card debt will become high.
- You love to borrow money and to take loans from the bank.
- Credit and owing others can be your downfall.
- You become angry and critical if someone owes you money.
- You look upon money as a power of influence and politics.
- You could end up paying lots of taxes and fees to court of government.
- You could lose money by robbery, thieves or fraudulent partners.

Money Code #7

- You're very secretive about money.
- Even though money may not be important to you, you need it.
- You spend lots of money on your parents.
- Using money for real estate is lucky for you.
- You do not like when other people owe you money.
- You become very emotional about your savings and your earnings.
- Raises and bonuses come to you slowly but surely.
- You do well in business money wise.

- You may secretly spend or earn money from bars or club-houses.
- Very few people know about your finance.
- You are lucky with the stock market and any farming business.

Money Code #8

- You like to spend money on quality and expensive things.
- Your extravagant taste makes you spend lots of money.
- Money passes through your hands very easily.
- Sometimes you spend money without worrying about other priorities.
- Many of you become models, fashion designers, actors or investors.
- Having a business of your own makes you earn a great deal of money.
- When you have a lot of money, you seek too much pleasure with the opposite sex, which eventually creates your downfall.
- Excessive abuse of power because of money can land you in jail.

Money Code #9

- Definitely a difficult money path is laid out for you in this life.
- You struggle to earn every dime in your life – learn to save.
- You'll be very fickle in your spending habits.
- Be careful of robbery or conflicts with others about money.
- Negative in your attitude towards money causes you to suffer court fines, medical costs, loss of savings and bankruptcy.
- Money kept in your hand is spent very easily.
- It seems you're always spending money to do all kinds of things without thinking of saving your money for hard times.
- Giving to charity as well as doing services for the poor helps you to generate lots of money; participating in temple activities benefits you.
- Working with the government relieves you of negative money problems.

CHAPTER 20

Equation # 19 – The Job Status Code

THE JOB STATUS CODE DETERMINES WHAT TYPE OF CAREER CATEGORY YOU WILL BE SUCCESSFUL WITH. IT IS OBTAINED BY ADDING YOU LIFE CODE TO THE JOB CATEGORY CODE AND THE RESULTING CODE IS CALLED THE JOB STATUS CODE.

Each one of us also has our career or job to make the Universe around us function and progress. We are made to fulfill a duty that will contribute towards the continuity of the Universe. Without work, the Universe cannot function.

Each element in the Universe is working constantly to keep the Universe alive. When we are given a job to do it is because that job was attracted to us through karma that was performed by our parents, grandparents and ancestors. For example, if you find your father or mother was involved in real estate sales at the time of your birth, then you also will be attracted to this type of career or job. If your father was a farmer at the time of your birth, you will possess an unconscious knowledge of farming.

Everything that happens to us between the age of 0 and 7 determines what type of career we will follow. A good look at the Hereditary Code (Chapter 9) may also indicate some of the characteristics that we learn from our parents at the time of pregnancy that will contribute to our choice of career. This factor and the other fact that our father or mother might have been involved in a particular type of career will influence our abilities and skills in the kind of career we will follow in our own life.

There are 9 main categories of career classification in the Universe. These are referred to as Career Codes, and they are as follows:

CAREER CATEGORY CODES

❖	REAL ESTATE AND LAND	= 4
❖	STOCK MARKET	= 4
❖	CONSULTANTS	= 5
❖	COURT AND POLICE	= 6
❖	COSMETICS AND BEAUTY SALON	= 8
❖	HOSPITALS & MEDICAL	= 7
❖	MORTGAGES & BANKS	= 4
❖	FARMING AND AGRICULTURE	= 4
❖	SHIPPING AND BOATS	= 9
❖	SHOPS AND STORES	= 8
❖	RESTAURANTS AND FOOD CATERERS	= 2
❖	MANUFACTURING AND BUILDING	= 4
❖	PUBLISHING & PRINTING	= 3
❖	MODELLING AND FASHIONS	= 8
❖	YOGA AND MEDITATION	= 3
❖	COMPUTERS AND TECHNOLOGY	= 7

Now add the category of career number to your *life code* to get the final code as your Job Code, for example if your lifecode is #5 and the category code is #4 then it is 5 + 4 = 9 which means you will not do very well as a farmer

NOW FIND YOUR JOB STATUS CODE AND READ IT BELOW:

Job Status Code #1

- Good, full of pressures and opportunities to get promoted
- May be promoted rapidly upward
- Will be given a lot of responsibility and leadership position
- Always will be asked to assist management
- This job will be good if you like to teach and lead others.

Job Status Code #2

- Your co-workers and managers will be excellent and cooperative.
- You will be liked favored by your managers and supervisors.
- You will be known as a dutiful and dedicated employee.
- You will feel comfortable with this job.

Job Status Code #3

- Many excellent and good opportunities for advancement
- Everyone will have a good sense of humor at the workplace.
- You'll find comfort in this job as a learning experience.
- This job may involve further training and knowledge.
- You'll get many raises and help.
- If in the media business you may travel a great deal.

Job Status Code #4

- A fair and hard working job with average pay.
- You could experience a lot of stress with this job.
- You will be constantly busy and always doing something.
- You may be working a lot of overtime on this job.
- The raises will come to you slowly but they will be good.
- Try to rest and eat properly while working this job.

Job Status Code #5

- You will experience constant changes and movement with this job.
- Your duties will be changed often by your bosses.
- Will be promoted and given raises often
- Learn to accept changes without question and your bosses will like you.
- This job may involve traveling, if so, do it.
- At this job you may be tempted to take home things from your workplace; try to avoid it.
- If you're a female you may experience sexual harassment by bosses.

Job Status Code #6

- You will find this job frustrating and full of responsibilities.
- There will be a fight for power between you and your co-workers.
- There will be many disagreements between you and the people of authority.
- Avoid participating with other coworkers in stealing or robbing the company.
- If this is a partnership, it will incur in serious disaster before being separated.
- Be careful of injuries or accidents on this job; your back may affect you while working.
- The best way to make this job positive is to perform all your duties with full dedication and learn to bow mentally to those in power.

Job Status Code #7

- Your work progress and promotions will be very slow on this job.
- Very few people will bother you on this job.
- If you start to move upward there will be jealousies by coworkers.
- You will be left alone to work by yourself most of the time.
- This job could require you to do a lot of analysis.
- Try to maintain a proper diet, as you may feel sleepy during working hours.
- Take time off to meditate sometimes.

Job Status Code #8

- Your place of work will be very extravagant and comforting.
- This job may involve the handling in lots of money or finance.
- The people around you will always be dressed richly in appearance.
- This job may involve a lot of people with ego.
- There will be a battle for power and money among the workers.

- You will receive constant raises and promotions at this job.
- If you're a female you may experience sexual harassment by bosses.
- To enjoy this job, help your employer make and save money.

Job Status Code #9

- Low pay, lots of tension and dissatisfaction will be the effect of this job.
- You constantly complain about the pay not being enough for the work.
- You may get into trouble because of confusion with orders and duties.
- You imagine that others do not like you; avoid this negativity.
- Be careful of injury, sickness or danger on this job.
- Someone with high ego may constantly harass you at this job.
- Raises are scarce but when you get them, keep quiet.
- Keep a low profile and avoid arguments and then you will be able to enjoy this job for a long time.

CHAPTER 21

Equation # 20 – The Mental Code

THE MENTAL CODE DETERMINES HOW YOU FEEL ABOUT OTHERS, WHAT YOU ARE WORRIED ABOUT MOSTLY AND WHT CAN MAKE YOU HAPPY OR UNHAPPY. THE CODE USED IS THE SAME AS YOUR LIFECODE NUMBER

The human body is unique in its fingerprints and in its voiceprint and each of us is different in appearance from other human beings. Our bodies inside contain energy sensors called *Chakras*. Each Chakra is like a generator that produces a unique feeling or emotion of its own in the body of that individual. These Chakras are like energy generators along our spinal column. There are nine Chakra generators within our spine stretching from the private area going upward all the way to the top of the brain forming the shape of a serpent. Sometimes this Chakra system is referred to as the "serpent energy" within us that creates our desires, feelings, emotions and, most important of all, our egos.

Modern doctors have not provided any real cure for depression OR MENTAL UNHAPPINESS, but rather have divided temporary relief in the form of tranquilizers and anti-depressants. These emotional disturbances cannot be controlled by drugs, but can be cured by changing the condition of our mind by watching carefully what we eat and drink. Just as alcohol can make you intoxicated, so also certain foods can make you depressed or happy and joyful. Caffeine is know be a natural anti-depressant food. Apple is a natural stomach acid cure and so on.

In the following paragraphs find your Mental Code and then in the next chapter find your meditation code to help you control the condition of your mind.

The Mental Code #1 – Your mind and your Emotion

- Your depression is linked to loneliness and rejection.
- You feel that no one cares about you and you are all alone.

- To cure this you need to meditate and pray, avoid too much drugs
- Find things to do on your own, projects that you will that will make you feel accomplished.
- It's possible you were abused at a young age; forgiveness is very important.
- Being a supervisor or boss makes you feel good in your life.

The Mental Code #2 – Your mind and your Emotion

- Your depression concerns your love life and gossip.
- You feel there is not enough love in you life.
- You get depressed when some one criticizes you negatively.
- If you are unable to find love or perform sexually you will be depressed.
- Watch what you say as this will help to cure your depression.
- Show your dedication by being subservient and you will receive attention.
- Cooperate with others always and offer to help; it will cure your depression.
- Pray that nobody takes advantage of your good heart…learn cooking lessons.

The Mental Code #3 – Your mind and your Emotion

- Your depression concerns children and control.
- You hate when you people do not listen or pay attention to you.
- Loss of a child or worrying about pregnancy depresses you.
- Reading, playing with children, babysitting or watching movies cures your depression.
- Accept the fact that you cannot get everyone to listen to you and take up writing, teaching or reading as a hobby.
- Having a baby cures your depressive moments.

The Mental Code #4 – Your mind and your Emotion

- Your depression is about job, career advancement and hard work.

- You think always that you are working too hard for too little pay.
- You tend to be stressed out and have problems with co-workers.
- Accept that jealousy from others is a good thing since it indicates that you are progressing in life.
- Perform your duties without question and you will get rewarded eventually.
- Try to relax and take a nap in the afternoon every day; it will help you.

The Mental Code #5 – Your mind and your Emotion

- Your depression is about the opposite sex, freedom to do things and being bored easily.
- Sometimes you think God is not watching so you try to break the rules of life.
- The result can land you in jail, trouble with family and denial of love from others.
- You worry about your sexual strength…you get depressed if impotent or frigid.
- If your freedom is restricted you get depressed, so avoid such situations.
- It's possible you were sexually abused as a child; seek counseling on this.
- Reading, traveling, writing, going to movies, and joining clubs will help to cure your depression. Keeping yourself busy helping others will bring joy to your life.

The Mental Code #6 – Your mind and your Emotion

- Your depression will be about family, your power, and your fears about separation and your status or position in life.
- You always have a fear of losing control to others and you fear the mysterious.
- It depresses you if your family rejects you or if you are losing in career or school.
- You like to be praised for your achievements; you hate changes in relationships.

- Realize that you can't control the Universe; it has laws which control you.
- Learn to bow and accept rules; before correcting others, correct yourself.
- Accept all responsibility given to you; learn to gain from each experience.
- You can become a great doctor, editor, lawyer or political leader...go for it!
- Learn to spend time and buy gifts for the family; it will cure your depression.

The Mental Code #7 – Your mind and your Emotion

- Your depression will be about your love life and your partner; avoid trouble by what you say and your connection with God or the Universe.
- You keep most of your feelings inside so this will increase your depression.
- Learn to speak out your feelings and express yourself outwardly.
- Becoming a radio announcer, a DJ or public speaker will help you.
- Addiction to alcohol and drugs will increase your depression.
- Whenever you are depressed you try to get intoxicated; avoid drugs.

The Mental Code #8 – Your mind and your Emotion

- Money, business, investments and lack of comfort depress you.
- You worry about your money, your assets and your appearance.
- You worry if your body is out of shape or if you are overweight.
- Joining the gym or exercise classes will help to cure your depression.
- You buy expensive things to impress the opposite sex; it's OK, go ahead.
- Acting in movies, taking up yoga or making profit in a business is good for you.
- Dressing up and pampering yourself with dining out and enjoying luxury satisfies your ego.

The Mental Code #9 – Your mind and your Emotion

- You are very susceptible to depression and are confused a great deal.
- You change your mind rapidly and can make those around you very confused.
- Because of your constant doubts and denial of things, you create your own depressive moments; try to accept all things as they are.
- Because money spends constantly in your hand you get broke easily; avoid impulsive buying.
- You struggle for everything in life because of your suspicion of others; you must learn to listen to loved ones and trust them.
- You must learn to bow to a higher power and become a student first before you can tell others what to do.
- You try to create exciting moments by accusing others in a sly way; prepare for the backlash.
- Bathing in the sea regularly and spending time at the beach will help you a great deal.

CHAPTER 22

Equation #21 – The Meditation Code

YOUR LIFECODE NUMBER IS THE SAME AS THE MEDITATION CODE NUMBER

The Vedic Code of Science views meditation as a science of mind over matter. The mind processes energy in the form of thoughts and creation. Its creative energy has the ability to create changes in the spiritual world. Because of the constant amount of energy used in the mind to control the body every so often our energy gets dissipated or highly negative. The negative energy of the mind can create health problems, which can cause malfunction of our physical body.

Have you ever noticed that when you meet certain people, they seem to have a calming effect on your mind while if you encounter certain others, the effect is very negative? Well, this is because of the energy field that is contained in the human body of one-person conflicts or merges positively with the energy field of the other person. As we go through our daily lives we come into contact with all kinds of energy levels or energy blocks. The food we eat, the clothes we wear, they way we sleep, the location energy of the places we visit all contribute towards our human energy aura. Whenever this energy aura around the human body is disturbed or irritated in a state of non-equilibrium, we experience low energy or the need to sleep longer. We also experience things like the inability to control our emotions, which may lead to anger, frustration and conflicts with others.

To repair auric energy around the body, the Vedic Code of Science recommends following the Meditation Code, which calms and repairs the broken parts of auric energy around the body. Each person has their own individual response to meditative energy and methods. The main cause of a person's problem with meditation is that most people think that they are able to control the Universe. Thus, they give up their faith in the fact that the Universe is more powerful than they are and do not recognize that the Universe is the higher power.

The first thing we should realize before commencing meditation is to accept the fact that the Universe is always alive and moving as energy around us. We must realize that we cannot change the movements of the Sun or the Moon or the planets or the wind or we cannot control the tides of the ocean. They control us; we have to conform to their rules. We must learn to bow and give up our ego with the thought that we think that we are in control but we are not. We must learn to bow gracefully to the Universe and realize also that we are but a speck in the solar system of the Universe.

In the following paragraphs, I have described the nine methods of Vedic meditation procedures that will help you to meditate in the appropriate way so that you can achieve the ultimate relaxation level in your life. Only one of the nine methods applies to your life according to your Life Code. The recommended techniques will help you achieve a maximum amount of positive energy from your prayers, meditation or yoga sessions.

In the following paragraphs, use your Life Code from Chapter 6 to get an idea as to how you should go about doing your meditation and controlling your own energy. The following paragraphs describe and recommend some meditation methods and techniques that you can use to guide yourself into proper meditation.

Meditation Techniques for Lifecode #1

- Your primary focus is on leadership and prestige.
- It is recommended that you meditate for a maximum of fifteen minutes. If you go any further than 15 minutes there may be difficulties with your mental concentration. To ensure concentration, be sure that you are alone and that you slow the racing of your mind. When meditating, try to think of all of the things that worry you and then try to find solutions to these worries.
- A quiet room in a building or a high platform is suitable for your meditation

Meditation Techniques for Lifecode #2

- Your primary mediation focus is on love, love connection and serving others.
- Learn to meditate on your spending and your desire for material things.
- Use your meditation moments for building your inner strength so that people cannot take advantage of your kindness.
- Learn to meditate on the people who return your love for them; do not try to buy anybody's love.
- All your prayers should be toward appreciating the simple things that people do for you.
- Do your meditation in a congregation or in a shrine or in front of an altar.

Meditation Techniques for Lifecode #3

- Your primary meditation focus is children, expression and social relationship.
- You should meditate and put light around your children instead of worrying about them all the time; your light protects them.
- You should meditate on changing your childish ways and think of those thoughts that make you mature in your thinking.
- In your meditation avoid ways of thinking how you can control others; instead see how much they love you.
- Remembering and replaying childhood fantasies makes you feel good in meditation.
- A nursery, in front of a television video for meditation or a school is good for your meditation location.

Meditation Techniques for Lifecode #4

- Your primary meditation focus should be on your career and home.
- Learn to relax in your meditation as you are always stressed at your workplace.

- You should learn to schedule yourself for daily meditation for at least 15 minutes; it will help your energy for love.
- When meditating try to cool off the anger you acquire during the daily schedule and learn to forgive.
- Underground caves and rocks on the ground are good places for your meditation.

Meditation Techniques for Lifecode #5

- Your primary meditation focus is change and sexuality.
- Remember that God is watching you at all times, so learn to obey the rules of the Universe.
- You must meditate carefully before you venture on any illegal acts, as karma surely returns the lash.
- Meditate on business ideas, strategies and inventions, as this will help you become wealthier.
- Choose an ocean or natural location for your meditation, as the energy will be better there.

Meditation Techniques for Lifecode #6

- Your primary meditation focus is responsibility, frustration and family.
- You must realize that you are not in control of the Universe; God is.
- It's very hard for you to meditate, because you do not like to give up control very easily.
- You may be too protective of your family so you must give this job to God and let Him do it for you in your meditation.
- You get frustrated very easily so you need to meditate to calm yourself down when you think you are losing control.
- A military base, government house or a temple are good locations for your meditation

Meditation Techniques for Lifecode #7

- Your primary meditation focus is love and godly things.
- It is recommended that you meditate for at least 30 minutes, so as to slow your thoughts. While meditating you should always be in the lotus position of sitting with folded feet,

with your thumb and forefinger touching. Your eyes should always be closed during meditation, as you are always looking at your inner self.

- A holy location, temple, mountain or place of worship is your best place for meditation.

Meditation Techniques for Lifecode #8

- Your primary meditation focus is wealth and luxury.
- It will be very difficult to meditate with your eyes closed; therefore it is recommended that you keep your eyes open during meditation. You meditate best when you have an object in front of you, such as a crystal ball or a candle.
- You must focus on the fact that money is not the source of happiness but inner peace is the greatest wealth.
- The more you meditate and pray so also your material desires are fulfilled.
- A monument, richly decorated room or building or office or work location is the best place for you meditation.

Meditation Techniques for Lifecode #9

- Your primary meditation focus should be on the struggle for progress, decision-making and health.
- Because of your confused state of mind, sometimes, you need to perform long meditation. Generally, half an hour to an hour is recommended. During this time, you are advised to calm your mind by having no doubts about the existence of God.
- Because of your changing beliefs, sometimes you accept the Universe and sometimes you don't. In your meditation session, learn to accept those things that you cannot change and change the things that only you have control over.
- Meditation is recommended for you at least twice a day, because you have the ability to absorb negative energy very easily.
- Your meditation area should consist of incense burning and a fountain or waterfall next to you. The best place for your meditation is on the beach or at the seashore.

- Meditation, yoga and prayers are important for you to remove health problems, doubts and denials.

Next to a river, on the beach, close to reservoir or in a processing plant, under a tree or in a lonely place are all good locations.

CHAPTER 23

Equation #22 – The Travel Code

THE TRAVEL CODE IS OBTAINED BY ADDING YOUR LIFECODE NUMBER TO THE DAY CODE OF THE TRAVEL DATE.

Back in 2009 June, French Airbus 330 left Brazil as Flight 447 headed for Paris, it never reached. Notice the lifecode #6 of the airbus itself and the flight number. (3+3+0 = 6 and 4+4+7 = 15 =6).

In addition to that it took off on May 31, which when added it's a 9 (5 +3=1 =9). A #6 flight taking off on a #9 day with 216 passengers, a #9 also (2+1+6 =9). Note also that the missing flight was recorded as 6/1/2009 which when added comes out to #9 (6 + 1 + 2 + 0+9) = 18 ➜ same as 666).

In addition to that the last Air France airplane crash took place when it was flight 4590 which is a #9 (4+5+9+0. That crash took place in July 2000. Previous to that there was another airline incident which happen on June 3, 1962, which is also a #9 (6+3+ 1+9+6+2 = 27 = 9)

For your information, these were the only plane crashes that France have had in its history. No other.

Another interesting airline crashes is Austria flight 2553 which is lifecode #6 (2+5+5+3) and the date was October 1997

A mathematical look at the Airline Flight numbers, the Airbus number, the day of the flight and the year the actual machine started flying can be a very useful warning when you are taking airplane flights for long trips. As you can see from the above the negative *life code*s of #9 and #6 can actually determine the success or failure percentage of the flight. When I first started traveling as a Swami, I traveled almost every week from Miami to New York as well as well as Toronto. At that time I did not check the dates before I made the reservations, and so when I would travel on my negative days I would not realize it until I reached the airport. On my #9 Life code days, the flights would be delayed for hours, and all my appointments would be cancelled and I would be changed to another seat or plane that was uncomfortable or hot. The negative flight numbers did not affect me as much as my day codes. After noticing this, I decided to check my reservation dates carefully and soon I realized that I had gotten very few delays and baggage problems. I had already lost bags and books and other items on negative *life code* days.

The equation for your Travel code days are compiled by adding your Lifecode number to the day code and the result is known as your Travel Code, for example if your date of travel is Jan 7 of the year , then add your Lifecode to the number 7. If your *life code* is a 5 then the result is $7 + 5 = 12 \rightarrow 1+2 = 3$ which is your travel code. Now look up the table below for good and bad travel days.

Travel Code # 1

- A *fair* day for traveling.
- Most likely you'll be traveling alone.
- You'll have lots of time to think and meditate.
- You may spend most of your time worrying about things in your life.
- Take a book, you may need it while traveling.

Travel Code # 2

- An *excellent* day for traveling.
- You may be traveling with a partner or family.
- You will enjoy the company that you are traveling with.
- Prepare to be talking or listening to music with someone.
- Dress well as you may be meeting people on your trip.

Travel Code # 3

- An *excellent* day for traveling.
- You may be traveling with children or young people.
- This may be an educational trip to a seminar or school project.
- You may be watching a lot of television or entertainment media.
- Take a notepad and book as you may be spending time writing or reading.

- Prepare to go to a party or social event on this trip.

Travel Code # 4

- A *negative* day for traveling.
- A hard and stressful day lies ahead.
- This trip may be job related or a business trip.
- If not job related, prepare to be tired at the end of your trip.
- You may be carrying extra luggage today.
- Make sure you take extra lunch and snacks as you may need them.
- Try to rest as much as you can after this trip.

Travel Code # 5

- An *excellent* day for traveling.
- This will be a fun trip or a vacation journey.
- Whether you're traveling alone or with others you will enjoy yourself.
- This may be a long distance trip or one out of state or country.
- You will return from this trip very satisfied and rejuvenated.
- Be careful of fraudulent contacts and deceptive agents.

Travel Code # 6

- A *negative* day for traveling.
- Whichever way you look at it, the trip ahead is rough.
- You may experience delays, additional costs and losses.
- Be careful of accidents if you're driving or of thieves if you're shopping.
- Prepare to leave home early so as to avoid delays.
- You may get frustrated and angry during the trip.
- A good advice is to accept all delays without arguments as this may be in your best interest; acceptance may save you from disaster.
- If you're visiting your family, prepare to have family disagreements after your trip
- Try to change your date to a good day for travel; it will help.

Travel Code # 7

- A *fair* day for traveling.
- Nothing exciting or interesting will happen on this trip.
- You will be doing a lot of inner analysis of yourself and your life.
- Take time off to meditate and plan your future well.
- Avoid getting drunk or intoxicated on this trip.
- You may encounter religious individuals or astrologers.
- Prepare to fall asleep sometime on your journey.
- Enjoy this quiet moment by yourself; you will feel rested at the end.

Travel Code # 8

- An *excellent* day for traveling.
- If this is not a business trip, it must be for pleasure indeed.
- Prepare to spend lots of money on this trip.
- If you're visiting casinos or gambling you may win.
- You may encounter beautiful and handsome individuals in your journey.
- Prepare to watch TV, look at fashions or enjoy great scenery.
- Business meetings and partnerships will be successful on this trip.
- Prepare to bring back lots of good stuff when you return.

Travel Code # 9

- A *negative* day for traveling.
- Whichever way you look at it, the trip ahead is rough.
- You may experience delays, additional costs, and losses.
- Be careful of accidents if you're driving or of thieves if you're shopping.
- This could be a journey to a funeral or hospital or a court.
- If you're traveling to a government center, prepare for delays.
- If your trip is changed without your control, do not protest as it may be for your own good.

- The location that you are leaving will demand you return to it soon.
- You may definitely have baggage problems, and additional expenses, so make sure you walk with extra money.

I hope that the above travel codes will guide you to make travel plans that will take you and bring you back safe from your journeys. Vedic Code of Science is recognized for its potential in preventing unfortunate and lucky occurrences in a person's life. Armed with the knowledge of this science, people can learn to travel safely.

The flight number of the Airline is very important. If the flight number adds up to 9, then there will be delays in the flight schedule, however there is no danger to the passengers on that flight , everyone will arrive safely. If the flight number is a #6 then there is some danger of breakdown or accident. However other factors must be taken into consideration when assessing the #6 flight. The best way to avoid all airline accidents is to get airline companies to avoid placing certain flight number on certain dates. If only they will listen to this knowledge many lives could be saved.

CHAPTER 24

Equation #23 – The Personal Home Code

THE PERSONAL HOME CODE DETERMINES YOUR SUCCESS OR FAILURE ENERGY AT THE HOME WHERE YOU LIVE . THIS IS OBTAINED BY ADDING YOUR LIFECODE NUMBER TO THE LOCTAION NUMBER OF THE HOUSE, RENTAL OR CONDO UNIT WHERE YOU LIVE. If your rental unit number is 3 and your lifecode # is 6, then the sum 6 + 3 = 9 = Your personal home code.

Now we will provide a description on how your life will be affected by the location or the place where you live. This will be revealed by the Personal Home Code.

Home Code#1 - Life in This Home

- You will feel independent, lonely sometimes and be bossy at home.
- You will achieve high status in career and position in life.
- You should be very spiritual in your thinking or you worry a lot.
- You love to advise others; people will listen to your advice.
- You will have a lonely child or you will feel pressured.
- You always feel that others leave you alone a great deal.
- Marriage partners are cautioned not to be too dominant.
- You may become too independent for your partner's feelings.
- You may worry a great deal; this may result in mental nervousness.

Home Code#2 – Life in This Home

- You like to shop a great deal and look for bargains.
- You cook tasty foods and food will always be in this house.
- You may have a job that involves cooking while living here.
- Make sure you serve all those who come here to reap good karma.

- Anyone who visits you and is fed will bless you with prosperity.
- You hate when your peace and quiet is disturbed in this house.
- People see you as kindhearted and too helpful to others.
- Others in the home will take advantage of your kindness.
- You will be involved in religious activities while living here.
- You will be involved in singing or may become a famous singer.
- Your partner in marriage makes a lot of demands for attention.
- You hate when anyone shouts at you here; it makes you angry.
- You will receive a lot of romance; too much for you sometimes.

Home Code#3 – Life in This Home

- Here you are usually skinny, small in stature and have a thin waist.
- You are argumentative and usually think you are always right.
- You may experience loss of children or have abortions in your life.
- Women here experience problems with regard to their uterus.
- They may also experience cramps, lower back pain or bleeding.
- You are childish in your ways; people think you are immature.
- You hesitate to accept responsibility but are forced to do it.
- You interact with the children a great deal.
- You may be involved in publishing, writing or selling books.
- Your career may involve some form of telephone communication.
- You have many telephone lines or sets in this home.
- There will be many computers or television sets in the home.
- You will be involved with videos, television and music publishing.
- You may lose weight while living here; you will look 10 years younger.
- You may have dental or plastic surgery done while living here.
- You will feel very comfortable and lazy while living here.

Home Code#4 – Life in This Home

- You will be very hardworking and conscientious while living here.
- You may have a high temper because of many stressful moments.
- You will be determined in your attitude and will not admit defeat easily.
- If you want something done, you'll pressure others to do it immediately.
- Too much work and overtime will affect your health.
- It may take you a long time to buy a home, as you save money slowly.
- Your income and expenses will most of the time be equal. Try hard to save.
- You are always busy doing something in this home; rest a little.
- Your mortgage may be high and your bills may be too stressful.
- Back pain and stomach problems will affect you from working.
- See the doctor regularly make sure your follow a spiritual life.

Home Code#5 – Life in This Home

- You will change your mind a great deal and quickly in this home.
- You love to travel and will travel to many places in the world.
- Because your thinking is fickle it's hard for others to know your thinking.
- You have intuitive powers and usually know things ahead of time.
- You will be able to tell if others are telling false things to you.
- You may be able know what others think about you by watching them.
- You will be helpful to others by self-sacrifice, forgiving enemies easily.
- You will help others without asking for compensation or money.
- You will have a psychic and profound connection with the Universe.

- You will counsel and advise friends and family in their business.
- You are not very lucky with relatives; family members have no appreciation.
- You will make friends easily; friends will help you the most in life.
- The more good actions in life, the more beneficial it will be for you.
- Being a vegetarian while living here will give you no health problems.
- You may experience problems with the government, IRS or immigration.
- While living here you will encounter many great spiritual personalities.
- You will own more than one vehicle while living here.
- Your job may involve traveling or driving long distances or using public transportation.
- You will receive many long distance telephone calls or contacts from overseas.

Home Code#6 - Life in This Home

- In this home you like to be in charge; you have a very strong ego.
- Your job will thrust many responsibilities upon you.
- If you fail to handle responsibilities while here, you will experience misery.
- You may experience a lower or upper back pain, headaches or migraines.
- Eating red meat in this home may lead to high blood pressure problems.
- If not working for the government, you may have government problems.
- Credit card problems, high mortgages and loans affect you here.
- Make sure you pay all bills by cash while living here; avoid credit.

- You may be able to have a business while living here; avoid loans.
- You refuse to accept astrology, the occult or God very easily. Pray.
- You feel very frustrated when you cannot have things your way.
- You will experience inner fears and may think there is no help from God.
- Avoid the color red or black as it brings surgery and health problems.
- You may experience police or court problems while living in this house.
- You could have many traffic tickets also while living here.
- Your marriage will experience family problems while living here.
- There will be fears of divorce or separation while living in this house.
- You could experience robbery or burglary while living here.

Home Code#7 - Life in This Home

- Your mind is running a thousand miles an hour while living here.
- Your mind constantly thinks and analyzes everything.
- You keep most of your thoughts to yourself; you hardly ever talk.
- You will not tell your plans to other members of the household.
- You feel you are right most of the time; you have a strong ego.
- You will experience jealousy; you may think everyone is against you.
- You appear very beautiful or handsome in the case of males.
- You appear very sexy and attract the opposite sex very easily.
- You have strong urges for love, sex and romance; you are very passionate.
- If your spouse is negative you will ignore him or her a great deal.

- A sure key to happiness for you is meditation, chanting and music.
- You will make a good radio announcer, singer or religious leader.
- You may become too kind hearted and will feel deceived by your lovers.
- You should avoid the colors black and red; wear light colors.
- You will become critical of others and gossip while living here.
- You may have a fear of spirits while living here in this home. Pray.
- You will meet many religious priests, psychics and astrologers while here.

Home Code#8 – Life in This Home

- You love money and constantly think or quarrel about it.
- You will have a business of your own at some point in this home.
- Money flows through your hands very easily; try to save some.
- If you are spiritual and conservative, the money will stay with you.
- You may purchase expensive items and will be attracted to luxury items.
- You will suffer from constipation problems and shortage of money.
- You may become involved in fashions, modeling or designing.
- You may have a strong ego and will feel that you are above others.
- Investments in the stock market may prove to be profitable.
- You will have money and will have people working for you always.
- You love jewelry and may own of lot of it. Silver and pearls are good.
- Avoid wearing anything black; this will kill your prosperity in life.

- You will be attracted to movies, yoga, stock market, etc.

Home Code #9 – Life in this home

- You may have a high temper or a suspicious mind while living here.
- You will experience the death of older family members.
- Be careful of accidents and traffic violations while living here.
- Alcohol will be very damaging to your life; avoid it in this home.
- You may think very deeply about life and may become religious.
- If you are positive person you could become popular or famous.
- You may become involved in politics or become a leader.
- You will become confused and will sometimes have many doubts.
- Working for the government will be very beneficial for you.
- You will struggle to fulfill your desires while living in this home.
- You will spend more than you earn and bring financial problems.
- You will be very fickle and impulsive in your actions in these houses.
- Negative husbands may abuse their wives physically and mentally.
- You will have a loud voice and will shout at others sometimes here.
- The key to your happiness – donate yourself to work for charity.
- You may spend your money without keeping some for the bills.

I hope each person, who has read the above, will use this information to help them buy the proper home by code so that happiness for the family can be experienced.

There are many times when a person has moved into a Building Code #9 home and has fallen ill immediately or a relative dies after the move. If you form a Personal Home Code of #6 or #9 with a building address, then it is advisable that you do not move in the home until you have consulted with a Life Code Advisor.

CHAPTER 25

Equation #24 – The Communication Code

THE COMMUNICATION CODE DETERMINES WHAT KIND OF MESSAGES WILL REACH YOUR EARS AND WHAT TYPE OF PEOPLE WILL YOU ASSOCIATE WITH THROUGH THAT MEDIA. HER THE EQUATION IS MADE FROM THE LAST 4 DIGITS OF YOUR PHONE NUMBER PLUS YOUR LIFECODE NUMBER.

The Area code of your phone number belongs to that area or state or county. The next three numbers after the area code is your exchange location code. In some countries these are sometimes 2 or 4 digits. The last four numbers are the numbers that identify you. This number determines how your phone will respond to all those who call you. Add this number to your lifecode number and the resulting number is the COMMUNICATION CODE with regards to your telephone. It could be a cell phone or home phone that you own with your name on the account.

If your phone number is 305 386 0308 then the last four digits are 0308. When added it becomes 11 and then reduced to 2 (0+3+0+8 =11$\rightarrow$ 1+ 1 = 2) . This is known as the Phone Code. Now if you check below it will tell you how the calls will come and from whom for the phone code.

Phone Code #1

This phone hardly rings. It will also be in a hidden section of the home

Phone Code #2

This phone rings a great deal. Most of the callers desire advice or help

Phone Code #3

Will ring a lot. Mostly young people and people who want to talk a lot

Phone Code #4

Will ring mostly from your job or medical people who are stresses. Some of the callers will call for unnecessary things

Phone Code #5

Busy with long distance calls. Possible pornographic or false sales people will call a lot. This phone will move around the house a lot

Phone Code #6

The callers will be family, quarrelsome people, creditors, government, police and court or legal personnel. Calls will be frustrating

Phone Code #7

This phone will be quiet, hardly ring and the callers can be religious, teachers, lecturers and priests. Negative callers are drug addicts, alcoholics etc.

Phone Code #8

Business callers, expensive phone, high class callers, gamblers and extravagant people such as investors, movie people, show biz etc

Phone Code #9

Distressed callers, sick callers, calls from across the ocean, calls from the hospital, calls from criminals

YOUR LIFECODE NUMBER + THE PHONE CODE = COMMUNICATION CODE

Now check the table above as to what experience you will have with the callers on your phone.

CHAPTER 26

Equation 25 – The Enemy/Friend Code

ADD YOUR LIFE CODE WITH THAT OF THE OTHER PERSON'S LIFE AND THEN YOU WILL BE ABLE TO DETERMINE IF IT'S A TRUE FRIEND OR ENEMY.

One of the most important things that we must realize is that jealousy can be a good thing or a bad thing. When a person is jealous of another person, it is an indication that the victim of the jealousy is really progressing in comparison to the aggressor, who may not be progressing. In other words, if you are the one receiving the jealousy from others, it is an indication that the person is jealous because you are progressing higher than they are. This is a good thing, as it indicates that you are doing well. However, sad to say, the people who may be jealous of you are suffering from the sickness of envy. When someone is envious of you, it means that they have too much ego thus this pride becomes their downfall. This jealous person has two choices: he can view you as the competition and try to strive higher or he can become negative and seek ways to bring about your downfall. If he chooses the latter then he may also bring about his own downfall.

Enemy Code #1

- These two individuals will not become enemies, but rather they will become competitors.
- They will always try to outdo the other person in everything.

Enemy Code #2

- They will never become enemies; they will always be friends.
- They will always love each other and consider one another's feelings.
- The only war they will have will be a war for attention from each other.

Enemy Code #3

- These two people are not enemies, but will have minor wars within their relationships.
- Childish behavior or words can create enmity among these two.
- There will be a battle for attention of other by both of the two.

Enemy Code #4

- These two will not become enemies unless the work together or live together.
- Friendship between these two without being attached to any material things will do well.
- There may be jealousy in the workplace that will be destructive.
- Coworkers may be competitive in their behavior for promotions.

Enemy Code #5

- Enmity is created in this relationship by distrust among these two.
- Both of these two people have a high degree of ego and pride.
- Neither of these two will admit that they're wrong, so that can create war.
- Sexuality may be a factor that creates enmity between these two.
- Each person wants to boss the other person around; this creates enmity.
- If one person restricts the other's freedom then there will be war.

Enemy Code #6

- There may be a dislike for each other from the time they meet.
- There will be a fight for power between these two constantly.
- They involve many others in their quarrel with each other.
- War between these two people breaks out very often.
- If these two cooperate they will become very powerful.

- Neither of these two admits that the other is right.
- They can become enemies and be at war all their lives.

Enemy Code #7

- A relationship that very rarely creates war unless there is extreme jealousy for each other.
- These two can be great religious and spiritual friends or extreme religious enemies.
- The egos of both are high and they can hate to the point of destruction through jealousy.
- Each person keeps their ill feelings of each other inside and then blows it all out one day creating war.
- Each person is attached to the other emotionally; prayer can help avoid war.

Enemy Code #8

- Money is the key factor that creates war between these two.
- Power, investments, stock market, business and more are factors that cause war between these two.
- Each person is competitive with the other in their achievements and watches each other carefully.
- Each person wants to look better than the other looks.
- Together if they cooperate they can make millions.

Enemy Code #9

- A relationship that can surely lead to war and destruction.
- Each person thinks and suspects the other of working against him or her.
- There will be constant arguments and war even though they love each other a lot.
- These two will end up in court surely if their fight becomes extreme.
- Money will be their destruction if loans are involved.
- Each one creates confusion for the other person.
- A third party is always required to settle the war between these two.
- They are always denying their faults with each other.

CHAPTER 27

Equation #26 – The Fertility Code

THE FERTILITY CODE DETERMINES YOUR LEVEL OF FERTILITY AND THE ABILITY TO PRODUCE CHILDREN. IT'S THE SAME AS YOUR LIFECODE NUMBER

There are many other factors that create infertility problems. Usually if these factors are corrected then the fertility level of the couple will be increased.

The following Life Codes (from Chapter 6) will indicate some possible measurement of the infertility level of the female or male involved. It will explain why some people are more fertile than others are. It also may help some of you understand why you are not able to get pregnant after trying so long. Finding out your Life Code and reading the following under your Life Code will help you apply to your life.

Fertility Code #1

- The fertility level is high and is considered positive.
- The chance of becoming pregnant is 80%.
- Most women of this category try to prevent pregnancy.
- The mother will feel confined when the baby is born.
- Because of the high fertility rate, young girls become pregnant easily.
- Some mothers may abandon their children at birth.

Fertility Code #2

- The fertility level is high and is considered positive.
- The chances of becoming pregnant are 100%.
- Most women with is Life Code usually do not like the labor pains and usually stop after 2 or 3 babies.
- Women consider child rearing a job too hard for them, however they make the best mothers.

Fertility Code #3

- The fertility level is low and is considered negative.
- The chances of becoming pregnant are 50%.
- Women in this category experience many uterus problems so fertility is low sometimes.
- They always experience a miscarriage or an abortion.
- Chances are the mother of this person experienced an abortion and miscarriage also.
- The more children they have the more prosperity.
- The males in this category will experience premature ejaculation problems.
- The women's wombs get twisted to the right easily thus causing infertility.
- Abortion of the 1ˢᵗ child can create infertility problems.

Fertility Code #4

- The fertility level is average and is considered fair.
- The chances of becoming pregnant are 70%.
- The women in this category will find some peace with themselves after childbirth.
- Usually they are very picky with their partners so children can come late in life.
- Any childhood sexual abuse usually lowers the fertility level of the women.
- These women form a deep spiritual bond with their children.

Fertility Code #5

- The fertility level is high and is considered positive.
- The chances of becoming pregnant are 100%.
- Most of these women experience some type of sexual abuse at a young age – if so, the fertility rate is lowered.
- If not, then the fertility rate is high and a pretty baby girl is conceived quickly.
- Abortion of the first child can prevent further conceptions.

Fertility Code #6

- The fertility level is low and is considered negative.
- The chances of becoming pregnant are 60%.
- Most women in this category will suffer from back pain; this will lower the fertility rate.
- Back pain or migraines may come from a childhood accident or fall and can causes a twisting of the womb.
- Red meat will also lower the fertility rate and cause miscarriages or inability to become pregnant.
- Avoiding all types of meat can increase fertility level.
- Massaging of the spinal cord can increase the chance of becoming pregnant.
- The men in this case experience low sperm count or weak erections.

Fertility Code #7

- The fertility level is average and is considered positive.
- The chances of becoming pregnant are 80%.
- Women in this category have weak wombs, which act dormant or barren sometimes.
- The reason for that is that there are more male hormones than female hormones in her body.
- Usually the hairier the body, the lower the fertility level, and the less hairy the more fertile she is.
- She must take hormonal treatment to increase estrogens.
- Special herbs can be taken to increase chances of pregnancy.
- Sitting in a tub of seawater can increase fertility level.
- Sit-up exercises or massaging of the lower belly with oils can increase the chance of pregnancy.
- Loss of head hair indicates low infertility.

Fertility Code #8

- The fertility level is low and is considered positive.
- The chances of becoming pregnant are 65%.
- The first being a girl most of the time the women experience many constipation problems.

- Women in this category tend to use a lot of contraceptives and usually when ready to get pregnant, the fertility level is lowered.

Fertility Code#9

- The fertility level is average and is considered positive.
- The chances of becoming pregnant are 70%.
- The women of this category can get pregnant easily provided no childhood abuse occurred.
- These are very energetic people who love to be with children always.
- The women enjoy being pregnant sometimes and experience pleasure from breast feeding their babies.
- The men in this category sometimes experience impotence or low sperm counts.

Please note that the female body contains its own fertility clock. After a woman has given birth to a baby, the impure blood continues to ooze out of her uterus for almost three months following the birth. She is usually infertile during that period of time. Also you must be aware that as long as the mother is breastfeeding the baby, the mother will not ovulate or menstruate until she stops breastfeeding the baby. As you can see, the female body has its own fertility control timer.

The Vedic Code of Science does not recognize menopause as a normal part of life. When a woman suffers from this complaint, it means that her womb has been affected by a sickness of some sort, and certain exercises and herbal treatments would be needed to fix the womb back into place so that the sexual sensitivity can be revitalized. In ancient times older women in the villages would treat women with this so-called "menopause" and wives would enjoy their husbands until they are way past the age of 60. So when the ovulation period stops, it does not mean the woman's love life is finished.

With regards to men, they will experience impotence or low sexual vitality if they do not eat a proper diet. Salt, onions, garlic, pepper and other stimulants will increase their energy for sexual attention. Herbs as well as all beans increase the chance of fertility.

CHAPTER 28

Equation #27 – The Pregnancy Code

THE PREGNANCY CODE TELLS YOU AHEAD OF TIME WHETHER YOUR 1ST CHILD WILL BE A BOY OR A GIRL. THIS CODE IS THE SAME AS YOUR LIFE CODE NUMBER. HOWEVER BEAR IN MIND THAT THE MARRIAGE CODE WILL AFFECT THIS OUTCOME ALSO.

Is it a boy or a girl? If you are wondering about the gender of your first, second or third child after you get married or pregnant, this chapter will provide you with interesting insight as to how you can determine this through the Vedic Code of Science. Nowadays, with the common use of contraceptives, pregnancy-controlling mechanisms and abortion clinics, many people have changed their views about pregnancy. Imagine if the entire woman decided to get an abortion, then what would happen to the world? There will be no continuation of the Universe. Each time a person has an abortion in the world; it changes the whole makeup of the Universe. The aborted child could be an Einstein, a Newton or a Christ.

The first pregnancy of a couple forms the first flower that will bear fruit in that couple's life. Usually, if the child is aborted, the couple will break up or separate. General statistics show that most young couples, who aborted their first child, ended up separating from each other after that. Most disabled children born to married couples are usually preempted by an abortion. It is as if the aborted child came back again to punish the couple for have aborted it. The disabled child becomes the punishment or the task of the whole family from grandmother to mother and whomever else.

We all know that once the seed is planted and starts to grow, the path of karma taken by that growth cannot be changed, just like shooting an arrow cannot be stopped or change its course once it leaves the quiver.

Nature and the Universe has also provided some type of guidance as to how we can determine how our future children are going to be, depending on the amount of boys and girls in the woman's life. This information can be found after the first child is born in the afterbirth that follows. The afterbirth contains ribbed parts of pink and blue. The number of pink and blue parts of the afterbirth indicates how many boys and girls are scheduled to born in the woman's life. If a child is aborted, the count is included in the afterbirth.

Doctors are not aware of this method of knowing how many children a person should have, however, it is an ancient knowledge, which has been used in India for centuries. In this writing, we will provide some of that knowledge according to the Vedic Code of Science. You can find your Fertility Code in Chapter 6 and use that code to find out about your children.

Pregnancy Code #1

- The first child will be a boy depending on the love connection. If the husband has a Life Code of #7, the first child will be a girl.
- If the first child is a boy, a girl will follow it.

Pregnancy Code #2

- It is most definite that the first child will be a girl. The only chance to a boy can occur if the husband is a Life Code 3.
- The second child will be a boy followed by a girl.
- You usually have a problem after having the third child and may refuse to have more because of the labor pain or pressure of pregnancy.
- Your children will protect you and take care of you later; you will benefit from them.

Pregnancy Code #3

- Definitely it's a boy no matter what the Life Code of the other partner is.
- Second child will be a boy if the first child was abortion or miscarriage.
- People with this Life Code always experience a Life code or miscarriage.
- If the first child is a boy and there is neither miscarriage nor abortions, it will be followed by a girl.

- The more children you have, the more prosperous your life will be.
- Usually there are more boys rather than girls.
- Most of the people in this Life Code may be denied children as a result of family background karma.

Pregnancy Code #4

- The first child is most likely a girl unless influenced by the other partners.
- The second child is most likely a girl followed by a boy.
- Girls are lucky for you and so there will be more girls than boys in your life.

Pregnancy Code #5

- The first child is most likely a girl unless influenced by the other partners.
- You love your children and will treat them like adults.
- Pregnancies are difficult and usually you may have only one son and many daughters.

Pregnancy Code #6

- The first child is most likely a boy if not influenced by partner's Life Code.
- The second child is most likely a girl followed by a boy.
- Most of the people in this Life Code may be denied children as a result of family background karma.
- Special methods and operations may be needed for pregnancy.
- Most of the people under this Life Code go through Caesarian deliveries.

Pregnancy Code #7

- The first child is most likely a boy if not influenced by partner's Life Code.
- The second child is a boy and could be followed by a girl.
- Most of the children may be boys.
- If the grandfather was abusive to women then all the

children will be just boys and no girls would be allowed in the family.

Pregnancy Code #8

- The first child is most likely a girl unless influenced by the other partners.
- Usually a boy may follow the first but most of the children are girls under this Life Code.
- Usually these couples only prefer to have only two or three children.

Pregnancy Code #9

- The first child is most likely a boy if not influenced by partner's Life Code.
- The second child is most likely a girl followed by a boy.
- Most of the children may be boys.
- There are possible abortions, miscarriages and difficulties with pregnancy.

There are many factors that may affect the outcome of a pregnancy. Vedic science teaches that the sex of the baby can be changed by spiritual words called "mantras" before the third month of pregnancy. In my work I have been able to help many women have children, even though the medical doctors had given up on them. I have also noticed that if the first child is aborted, the child following may become disabled for some reasons.

It is advisable that the first child should never be aborted, as this pregnancy is the planting of the first seed, so to speak, and is the first flower of love that comes from the newly married lovers. The first baby will contain the essence of their love connections.

In my experience, I have also noticed a hereditary trait that affects the outcomes of pregnancy and that is that if a female child was abused, molested sexually or if she eats a great deal of red meat then the womb somehow becomes traumatized. Thus, she is unable to become pregnant after she gets married. In addition, if the father of any boy was a sexually illicit or perverse person, his sons will be denied female children.

My advice is always to make sure you check your family history thoroughly before assessing why you may be having problems with pregnancy.

CHAPTER 29

Equation #28 – The Love (Dating) Code

THE LOVE CODE IS DETERMINED BY ADDING THE
LIFECODE NUMBERS OF BOTH PARTNERS AND OR
LOVERS AND THE RESULTING NUMBER IS THE LOVE
CODE.

LIFECODE OF PARTNER A +
LIFECODE OF PARTNER B =
THE LOVE CODE

Love code #1

- Not a good love connection; it is considered fair but negative.
- This connection could fail as a result of loneliness by each partner.
- Each lover makes the other one feel rejected.
- Seek advice before getting married.
- If this love connection leads to marriage it's because one partner does not want to let go of the other, which may result in separation mentally and also through illicit affairs.
- Worrying and loneliness will have to be the acceptance for both partners before they can be happy.
- Warning – If one partner is abusive in this connection, then marriage should be avoided.

Love code #2

- An excellent combination for love connection.
- What and how they speak to each other is important in the love connection.
- Romance, music and food will determine the success of the love connection.
- Love connection will last a long time and it will definitely lead to a happy marriage life.

Love code #3

- An excellent combination for a love connection.
- Childish and immature quarrels can lead to divorce or separation.
- If the partners don't have a sense of humor it will lead to disaster.
- Children and childish ego control by one partner can destroy this marriage.
- Any abortion prior to the marriage will destroy the relationship.
- This love connection will result in marriage and the wedding will be like a great party.

Love code #4

- Not a good love connection; it is considered fair but negative.
- This love combination needs a lot of effort to make it successful, as each partner will suffer a lot of stress from each other.
- Career choices and hard work will be the factors for happiness.
- This connection will lead to marriage.
- Because of stress each partner should try to look after each other's health.

Love code #5

- An excellent combination for a love connection.
- Extramarital affairs or each partner not wanting to be wrong can destroy this love connection.
- This connection may not lead to marriage as a result of distrust.
- Each partner must learn to trust each other before marriage.
- Sexual encounter will occur prior to marriage.
- A decision for marriage may come up too early.
- If each partner does not try to overtake each other's freedom the love connection will become fruitful.

Love code #6

- This is a negative love connection combination and must be carefully monitored.

- Family is the greatest trouble & blockage if allowed to interfere in their lives.
- This love connection may not lead to marriage as a result of family interference.

Love code #7

- A good love connection that can be destroyed by ego.
- Each partner is looking for a perfect spouse and there is no such thing as a perfect person.
- This can lead to love connection but a lot of effort is needed for communication between the two.
- This connection will lead to marriage and can become very happy if the partners are very spiritual.

Love code #8

- An excellent combination for a love connection.
- Money, luxury, and investments will affect this love connection.
- The wedding ceremony will be of grand scale.
- Extramarital affairs or each partner not wanting to be can destroy this love connection.
- This connection will lead to marriage and can be very happy.

Love code #9

- This is a very negative love connection combination and must be carefully monitored.
- This love connection is not recommended unless proper precaution is taken.
- Death of a family member, sickness, and financial problems are all factors that can follow this combination.
- For the love connection to work properly each partner will have to be vegetarians, avoid alcohol and bath in ocean waters frequently.
- This connection may not lead to marriage but if it does it may become a health-affected relationship.

CHAPTER 30

Equation 29 - The Love Day Code

THE LOVE DAY CODE DETERMINES WHEN IS THE BEST DAY TO GO OUT ON A DATE, GET MARRIED OR GO ON A HONEYMOON. THIS IS OBTAINED BY ADDING THE LIFECODE OF THE PERSON(S) INVOLVED TO THE DAY NUMBER. IF THE RESULT IS NEGATIVE THEN ANOTHER DATE MUST BE CHOSEN.

WHAT ARE THE BEST DAYS FOR LOVE AND ROMANCE?

NOW READ THE FORECAST FOR THAT LOVE MAKING DAY IN THE FOLLOWING PARAGRAPHS

LOVE DAY CODE # 1

- o A fair day for love making
- o If there are no ego and feelings of rejection lovemaking will go well today
- o You will feel aggressive and dominating in your sexual needs and desires
- o You may not be able to concentrate fully as you will worry about things
- o Avoid being too dominant , do not rush the lovemaking session today

LOVE DAY CODE # 2

- o Excellent and positive day for lovemaking
- o If male you will find that you are having an erection almost all day
- o Your feelings of love are strong and may want to go more than once
- o The opposite sex will look beautiful and attractive to you today

o You may meet many friends of the opposite sex today

LOVE DAY CODE # 3

o Not such a great day for lovemaking but good for playing with each other
o You may enjoy good sex if your partner is running a good day
o You may find yourself losing interest in the middle of the session
o You may find yourself getting too excited so that you finish too quick
o More foreplay should be done and a massage to your partner is suggested first
o If you are looking to get pregnant, this is a good day – fertility is high
o Looking at x-rated movies with your partner will help a lot today
o You love to hear sexy talking and funky words from your partner

LOVE DAY CODE # 4

o A difficult day to make love, lots of effort will be needed
o Tempers can flare and stop the desire for love, do not get angry
o Lots of effort will be needed by you to please your partner
o Your mind could be on your work instead of sex today
o If you have to make love today, relax first , avoid stress and then do it

LOVE DAY CODE # 5

o EXCELLENT DAY for lovemaking and great sex
o You will be feeling very sexy and ready today
o Provided you partner is on a good day, you will have fun in lovemaking
o Try to make it last as long as you can as it will be fulfilling
o If male your erection will be coming often, fantasies will be good for you

- o If male all the women will look sexy to you, if female vice versa
- o You will come into contact with attractive people of the opposite sex

LOVE DAY CODE # 6

- o A NEGATIVE DAY for lovemaking and partnership fun
- o You find yourself frustrated by the opposite sex today
- o You may lose the desire for sex quickly while making love
- o Your partner may not be ready when you are and you may be disappointed
- o If your partner refuses to be with you in the morning,, try again later
- o There may be interruptions from family members causing no sex for today
- o Interruptions can come from phone calls etc causing a lack of concentration
- o You and your partner may have a fight/quarrel thus killing the desire for sex
- o Usually lovemaking after a fight today may make the session more passionate

LOVE DAY CODE # 7

- o Deep Lovemaking full of desire and fantasies today
- o As a female, being naked and or scantily clad for your partner is good
- o You may wish to do a striptease dance for you partner today , it will help
- o Sexual desire is strong and lovemaking should be slow and sure
- o Looking at sex or love movies will help you fantasize more with your lover
- o Short dresses and tight clothes will stimulate your partner very quickly

LOVE DAY CODE # 8

- An excellent day for lovemaking and for enjoying each other's body
- Dress up sexy today as your partner is looking for beauty and poise
- Spend some money with your partner, go to dinner, give a gift
- You are looking to go out today around the town and then a sexy night
- You will feel good if you make money today, you will want to make love
- You enjoy a clean and luxurious environment, a hotel is good for sex today
- Pamper yourself , you will meet attractive and sexy looking individual
- You could meet prostitutes, strippers or actresses today
- If sex is in your karma today, it will be after you spend some money

LOVE DAY CODE # 9

- A CONFLICTING DAY for sex and love, Good if it happens…good if it don't
- This can be an extremely enjoyable day for sex or a negative day for it
- You will be feeling very sexy today or very exhausted also if negative
- If lovemaking is done, it will be very passionate, if not its also good
- You may be feeling sexy but your partner will not be, you will have to try hard
- If the marriage is negative you could find yourself sleeping in another room

CHAPTER 31

Equation 30 - The Sexual Code
The Cause Of Human Creation

Like every creature, humans have received certain rights and certain duties for a successful existence in the world. Objects of comforts have also been provided. For human beings there are four objects for his existence. These are religion, luxuries, carnal pleasures and salvation. Most people neither crave nor strive for all four. The first three – religion, luxuries and carnal pleasures – are more important for them. These three objects are the basis of the word called love and are the basis for reason of existence. Everybody strives to achieve any of these objects with all his or her might. The discipline of love is a very difficult one to achieve and very hard to understand without the proper knowledge provided by the Vedic Code of Science.

Despite having enthusiasm, determination, faith and capacity, often a human being fails to achieve his object for the want of a competent partner. Sexual pleasure or carnal pleasure is one of the main objects of existence of a human being. But without a well-laid discourse and discipline, no one can achieve the best satisfaction in this pleasure. Like other disciplines, the Code of Love also contains certain norms and disciplined actions necessary to achieve one's goal.

Like religion and earnings, sexual satisfaction or carnal pleasure is the third goal of human life. Without having a proper knowledge of the Sexual Code, one cannot experience all the other physical comforts. A married person is naturally inclined towards carnal pleasures. In other words, carnal pleasures constitute the basic reason for marriage.

A man and a woman agree to tie a nuptial knot not only to have carnal pleasures but also to reproduce and provide continuity to the Universe. Marriage simply reflects the social nod for their union. The legal contract for the marriage only is an illusion. The real marriage takes place when the couples have been consummated sexually. The first date they make love with each other is considered the first day of marriage. Each time a woman makes love to a new man he is considered to be her husband in God's eyes. There are no city halls in heaven. A person entering a sexual union without knowing the basic knowledge about it, they will not be able to achieve the basic goal of marriage. It is here where The Vedic Code of Science comes in the picture. Evidences show that a sexual union of male and female forces had never been taken for granted even in ancient time. Ancient literature describe profusely about the authenticity, necessity and relevance of the Vedic Science of Sexual Codes and the necessity for sexual disciplines.

Necessity of Education in Love Codes

The intelligent man in the olden days could enter married life only when he had thorough knowledge of Love Codes. His married life as result would be free from problems and conflicts.

Physical intimacy and sexual relations comprise the most delicate part of all human relations. In the words of well-known author, love seems to be the fastest thing, but it is the slowest thing to grow. Nonetheless, millions of people unite every year with the opposite sex. Some of these partnerships last a lifetime.

This section describes the kinds of the partners and agents who assist them in contracting with each other and establish physical relations

Categories of Male and Female Partners

According to the size and depth of their private organs, male and female partners have been put in 9 categories according to the Life Codes (from Chapter 1).

Rabbit, Snake and Bird males usually have a small phallus or in the case of females, small vaginas. Deer, Lion and Cow males have normal size phalluses and in the case of females, average vagina sizes, while Horse, Elephant and Tiger males have extremely large phalluses and in the case of females, deep or large vaginas. This information is very helpful when matching the marriages or sexual partners, as you can see if a Deer is matched to a Lion, it can be disastrous. Similarly if a Rabbit is matched to a Tiger it can be destructive.

TABOOS IN PHYSICAL RELATIONS

Of course, there is a strong attraction among the members of the opposite sex. This drive urges human beings to establish close physical contact with the opposite sex. But it won't be wise to have a physical relation with just anybody. There are certain taboos that give this behavior a direction, which a person should follow for saving themselves from sickness, death and suffering. According, one should avoid physical relations with the woman, who feels that she is better than all others or to a very low class woman, who is unclean and has bad habits. One should not long for a lustful relationship with a woman married to someone else. One should not have a relation with a woman who has been condemned by the societies, for it will damage your reputation.

Sound mental and physical health is the foremost necessity for establishing an intimate contact. A satisfactory physical relation between husband and wife is, in fact, the basis of a happily married life. Medicines are therefore required to remove physical ailments. Sages have developed certain Vedic of Science Remedies along with many herbal preparations to correct common physical ailments that lead to impotency in males and frigidity in females.

Lack of love and understanding between husband and wife is the most common mental problem that haunts most couples. Without love, no physical contact can bear fruits no matter how intimate it is. Hence, mutual love and understanding is also necessary to achieve peace in married life. Here, spiritual measures come in the picture.

Kinds of Lovers and Partners

For the purpose of procreation and continuity of the Universe, female partners are created with sexual attraction in mind. The woman's body is the objective desire of every man. Even wise sages and ancient Gods fell prey to the beautiful and scantily clad women enchanted by lustful desires. There are mainly 9 kinds of male and female partners. These are determined by the Life Codes.

The Prostitute Lover falls in the 8th, or 6th or 9th category above. The Single and Widow Lovers can be the 1st or 7th or 9th category and the Dedicated Partners can be mostly 2nd, 3rd, 4th or 5th categories. Please note: I said Dedicated Partners not Lovers, as a woman or man may still be a dedicated partner, but if he or she does not get enough sexual attention at home then having a sexual lover outside the marriage is not completely ruled out.

Men must also take notice that if a woman is a widow, the Vedic Code of Science advises that her second or third husband or lover will die also, since there are planetary afflictions located in her uterus area for a long period of time. The spouse must also remember that the lovers in the 1, 6, 7, 8 and 9 categories are always in need of sexual attention and if not provided will look for other lovers.

Hence, in the next chapter, The Vedic Code of Science presents an ideal method of assessing your sexual compatibility using the Sexual Compatibility Code and a way to understand how you can please your partner with complete satisfaction by understanding their sexual needs and fantasies.

CHAPTER 32

Equation 31 -
The Sexual Compatibility Code

Using the Vedic Code of Science we can add the Life Codes of the two people and obtain the Love Code to determine how the couple will enjoy their lovemaking sessions. Again, from Chapter 6, take your Life Code and add it to your partner's Life Code. For example if your Life Code is #5 and your partner's Life Code is #2 then adding the two will result in a Love Code of #7 (5+2).

Sexual Compatibility Code #1

1-9: In conjugal relationship, the sensual aggressiveness of the #1 man matches the passion and submissiveness of the #9 woman. If the man is #9, he is impulsively passionate and the inventive and demonstrative. A #1 woman will match him perfectly.

2-8: When the man is #8 and the woman is #2 adjustment would be better if they reversed their roles. The tough and practical #8 man pursues a life of material satisfaction and the personality of the soft and cooperative #2 woman remains eclipsed. She does not quarrel and is happy with taking the backseat when he shows love and affection. She likes the protection and security provided by her partner.

3-7: Sexually, it is surprising to find #7 not reserved but a sensual and demonstrative person. The #3 is known to be warm and passionate and should enjoy the ecstasy of lovemaking very much. Inventions of #7 and impulses of #3 make them a well-matched team in the game of love.

4-6: #4 and #6 are fairly compatible in sexuality. Concerning their love life, both are generous, faithful, considerate and romantic rather than give away to animal passion. There is a satisfaction and happiness for both of them. #6 is more inclined toward lovemaking and #4 is fully supportive.

5-5: With regards to #5 and #5. The two #5's put together will be the worst possible combination and should be avoided as much as possible whether in personal life or in business. Each one of them has a love for freedom and cannot have parallel thoughts. Both of them are highly-strung, changeable and restless. If they live or work together, a disaster is imminent. Sexual attention becomes difficult even though both want it all the time, they cannot agree because of ego.

Sexual Compatibility Code #2

1-1: Both persons have the nature of leadership and self-concern. Each one may try to outdo the other in a never-ending game and it is anybody's guess who will be the winner. The solution can be found in compromise and cooperation by dividing the duties and privileges etc. This would be easier in a business partnership but not so easy in love and marriage where both have the prestige of their jobs on the one hand and dealing in household chores on the other. They may make an allowance for freedom to each other as far as seeking pleasure is concerned and won't be much worried about what that the other one is doing and where.

2-9: Both of them are imaginative, charitable, faithful, kind and affectionate. The inferiority complex of #2 is nicely covered and positive by the charm and forgiveness of #9. The #9 abides nicely with the suspicion, moodiness, sensitivity and creativity of #2. Impulsiveness and being prone to accidents are the negative points of #9, but the #2 learns to live with them. They enjoy conjugal bliss, share beautiful thoughts and enjoy each other's company. Passionate 9 longs for making love and #2 cooperates fully.

3-8: The two of them have personalities with serious differences and frequent chances of clashes. Both of them are ambitious but #3 is easygoing and not serious. On the other hand, no man in general and #3 in particular would be able to tolerate the authority of the #8 woman. On the intimate side, #8 is strong in lovemaking and #3 is warm, impulsive and adventurous. But #8 is jealous and moody and

#3 can have extramarital relations if #8 is non-cooperative for very long.

4-7: A very good combination because of the balance in their natures. Both of them are calm, good-natured, non-argumentative and pleasant in their dispositions. Number 4 is practical, hardworking and trustworthy, providing security to the #7 woman, which she loves. On the intimate side they are found to be so well matched at all levels of expression – mental physical and spiritual – that perhaps they enjoy maximum ecstasy in lovemaking compared to any other couple.

5-6: One of them is hot tempered while the other one is of a cool temperament and consequently they seem to improve in time. The #5 may take risks, traveling, meeting people, given to pleasure of life, and try to convert the clever-minded impulsive #6 into accomplishing worthwhile goals. In their private life, #6 is loving and considerate but not sexually inclined. On the other hand #5 is more sexually inclined and insatiable, whether male or female. Either #6 has to fully cooperate with #5 having no personal demands or turn a blind eye towards its extramarital relations. It may be possible, if #5 is the male but perhaps difficult it is the female. This is the negative side of their relationship.

Sexual Compatibility Code #3

1-2: An ideal combination, especially if the man is #1 and the woman is #2, drawn to each other as opposites attract. The #1 man is dominating while #2 woman is submissive and they complement each other very well. The #2 woman is romantic, loyal, a born hostess, passive and always willing to do what a man wants. She will wait for him in the evening, look after him and give him conjugal bliss and assist him in all family dealings. She too is quite content because he gives her whatever she wants. She should not give chance for jealousy or provocation by her behavior otherwise there can be serious problems.

3-9: A very good combination of odd numbers leading to a successful union. Both of them have charm, which attracts each other. The #3 man at times can be obstinate and bossy but the #9 woman is tactful enough to handle him. Their conjugal bliss is perfect since both of them are romantic, warm and passionate and they like each other. They would never like to be separated from each other.

4-8: Both of them have similar viewpoints in life – practicality, hard work, intelligence, calmness and an urge to make a very good material and financial base for their lives. They make a successful team, achieving a lot in life, provided #8 does not push #4 too hard. Number 8 at times can be selfish, aggressive and might consider quarreling as normal. Number 4 is reliable, calm and charming. The bullying, cajoling and love of luxury and grand life style of the #8 may upset and disturb the #4 beyond repair, and this combination can result in failure. Number 8 is loyal and devoted but on the surface it finds difficulty in the expressing emotion or affection. At times it is moody and possessive and can hurt the feelings of the systematically affectionate and calm #4. Only occasionally can they make love to each other with satisfaction. This is a sore point in their relationship.

5-7: One thing, which both of them like, is to travel – a common factor, while in all other departments they must have a working compromise for successful living.

6-6: An ideal pair, completely in tune with each other, demonstrating love, beauty, happiness and a completely balanced family and home life. They do not need a probation period to decide on marriage. Their intuition tells them that they are made for each other. In lovemaking, they have better satisfaction in admiring, showering affection and caring for each other rather than getting involved in physical union every time. But nonetheless they enjoy perfect conjugal bliss.

Sexual Compatibility Code #4

1-3: Number 1 and #3 are quite suitable to each other and they should make a good couple. The #1 man has leadership qualities whether at work or in the home. He would like his mate to be smart, well dressed and charming, which the #3 woman is. She is talented and versatile and is very well satisfied with the masculinity of the #1 man. If the man is #3 and the woman is 1 they make the same good couple with slightly interchanged roles. Both of them are lively and intelligent and can share very well the thoughts and feelings of each other.

2-2: Made for each other, identical in most of the ways, this combination is a symbol of perfect happiness. They would never like to away from each other even for short periods as they both like sex all the time at the least opportunity they have…if they do not have a quarrel. They enjoy a conjugal relationship. Both of them are romantic and compassionate, enjoying each other's company as they enjoy their sexuality.

5-8: A very strong combination – #5 is adventurous, resourceful, and impatient, while #8 is materialistic, practical and strong.

4-9: On the personal side they make a slow but well developed relationship. Both of them are patient, understanding, compassionate and idealistic. In other respects they suit each other well. Number 4 can teach practically, hard work, and reasonableness in emotions and handling of money with care. Number 9 can teach spirituality, large mindedness, philanthropy and development of creative ideas. Number 9 is romantic, impulsive and demonstrative while #4 is systematic and orderly although loving and considerate but not adventurous. Hence if #9 learns to keep in check and is careful, the two of them will experience happiness and great joy in lovemaking.

7-6: The relationship is not a promising one if the man is 6 and the woman is #7. The #6 man is artistic and loving and looking for closeness and companionship. He would like to start the day with an affectionate kiss and would like to see his partner waiting for him for a warm fondling and a kiss when he returns home. When the man is #7 and the woman is #6 the situation is reversed with respect to their roles. The #7 man is imaginative, studious, philosophical, good-natured, dignified, and does not care for material or financial status very much. He finds a complementary union with the peaceful, quiet, loving and home loving #6 woman. Both of them are attracted to each other and they make a happy couple. Number 7 is the masculine number suited to a woman. They do surprisingly well with each other. Passionate and demonstrative, #7 man and romantic though spiritual #6 Woman enjoy their copulation.

Sexual Compatibility Code #5

1-4: This relationship is not recommended due to conflicting personalities and different views and opinions, and the compatibility is not likely to be there. There will be distrust and false accusations most of the time. They are generally indifferent in sex. Sex will be their downfall. The #1 woman likes a lot of excitement and adventure while the #4 man is the reverse.

2-3: The #2 man is kind, thoughtful and always willing to adjust and help. The two of them will start on a harmonious note and the going is good. But with the advancement of time, the #3 woman will find her beyond his limits, proud, independent, and definitely suspicious her of extramarital relations. And the #3 woman at no cost is going to bear the accusations. The relationship is not likely to last long. In case the man is #3 and the woman is #2, the combination is likely to be good and lasting, with their roles interchanged. The #3 man will easily have his way to find #2 woman to be good for him since she is timid, loving and perfect housewife. For her, he is a he-man giving her complete satisfaction. On the intimate side, one of them is romantic and tender (2) while the other is charming, versatile and warm (3) and the two complement each other very nicely. Although the physical side of the union may not be important for them, they will still have a regular sex life with each other.

5-9: A partnership that can be very good at times and very bad on other occasions. Whenever it is the good, the credit goes to the visionary, spiritual and determined to live for others (#9). And whenever there are differences and problems it is due to the excited, high strung and self-indulgent #5. Number 5 should check its impulses and #9 its prejudices and moodiness. The sexy and adventurous #5 and emotional, passionate and visionary #9 should enjoy the ecstasy of copulation except when they feel out of sorts, because there might be disastrous nights.

6-8: The home loving #6 man and career-minded and materialistic #8 woman can strike a working balance if they accept each other's nature as such. The #8 woman is ambitious, strong and will do anything to achieve worldly things, money and power. The #6 man is quiet, loving, peaceful, artistic and creative. If both of them agree to his staying at home and her working anywhere in the world, including late hours at times, then the relationship can be successful. But the #6 man can be jealous and suspicious. Number 6 is the lover while #8 is moody and needs coaxing for lovemaking. Moreover, #8 is jealous and possessive but the smothering treatment of #6 brings the best out of it and they are likely to enjoy their copulation. The credit goes to the tolerant and affectionate #6, whether man or woman.

7-7: Both of them think, act and feel in the same way, completely in tune with each other, forming a stable and harmonious relationship. Both of them are brilliant, peace loving, non-argumentative, philosophical and studious. At times, they can be optimistic and confusing because of laziness or aloofness. On them intimate side, both of them are imaginative, demonstrative and passionate. There is neither suspicion nor jealousy, and they are in tune with each other. They enjoy lovemaking on the mental, physical and spiritual planes equally. There is happiness and bliss between them.

Sexual Compatibility Code #6

1-5: The two cannot go together for a long time. Number 1 is determined steady and career minded while #5 is versatile, changeable and sexy. The relationship is still worse when the man is 1 and the woman is #5. The #5 woman does not marry early in life unless she has had pre-marital relationships. It is only their private life, which may keep them together if they can compromise on other issues. The #1 man is strong, demonstrative and adventurous while the #5 woman can adjust in matters of sex. So the two can be suited to one another. If the man is #5 he is more prone to sex but the 1 woman too can adjust and the two can make a good couple.

3-3: Both of them are talented, versatile, and lively but restless and cannot settle down. They are proud, do not like to be obligated to others, are outspoken and love personal freedom so much that any joint venture appears a limitation and is likely to be unsuccessful. In private life, both of them being passionate and impulsive, enjoying conjugal bliss galore though neither of them is jealous or possessive of the other. Family members interfering in their private lives will constantly haunt them. They will long for some sex time and will hide to get some privacy.

2-4: A destructive and sometimes unbalanced relationship brings out the worst in each other. The #2 man is sometimes shy and diplomatic, and likes to avoid conflict at any cost. The #4 woman is practical, a born organizer, and is sometimes cold and cheap. She will, however, save for the future. When it comes to sexuality, the #4 woman can be very cold and unemotional towards her partner. The #2 man demands a lot of sexual attention, and the #4 woman refuses to provide that attention as much. This may result in the separation of beds or a divorce. Both individuals in this relationship may have been previously married. For this marriage to work, both partners need to put their egos in check and avoid involving family members in their affairs. The #2 man is shy, diplomatic and likes to avoid conflicts at any cost. The #4 woman is practical, a born organizer, calm and would adjust her budget according to the salary of #2 man knowing that he is not earning well. She will save for the future, too.

6-9: A well balanced relationship, both of them being artistic, talented, loving, tolerant, and understanding of each other's needs. It is a rare combination of beauty, domesticity, trust and devotion on the one hand of #6 and high mental and spiritual power, truth, philanthropy and love of mankind on the other #9. They should make a wonderful team because they understand each other at all levels of consciousness. They find enjoyment at both levels of consciousness-spiritual and physical. Both of them are romantic, patient, and considerate but with greater emphasis on the mental union rather than the physical. Nevertheless, #9 is passionate and impulsive while #6 is warm and affectionate, and there should be a tint of happiness and fulfillment in their copulation.

7-8: Number 8 is strong, ambitious, career-minded, and will not settle for anything until power and position is attained. Number

8 is resourceful, self-disciplined, ruthless and aggressive and can be selfish under negative circumstances. Number 7, on the other hand, is intuitive, studious, non-materialistic, meditative, and more often than not would try to adjust with the hot temperament of #8. Number 7 can be aloof and secretive, raising suspicion and jealousy about involvement and whereabouts in the mind of #8. By nature, #8 is moody, living in extremes by luck. In copulating there can be serious ruffles if #8 is jealous and suspicious. But the emotional and passionate #7 can coax and bring about a harmonious sexual relationship if the #8 is in an extremely cold mood.

Sexual Compatibility Code #7

1-6: A balanced and well-adjusted couple that complements the needs of each other. The #1 man is demonstrative and adventurous while the #6 woman is romantic and chivalrous, and the two adjust well to each other's needs. If the man is #6, he is romantic and demanding while the affectionate and demonstrative 1 woman adjusts.

3-4: There are personality clashes between the two and a lot of allowances and compromises are necessary if the relationship is going to stay. It will depend on how much they can care for each other. In arguments, #3 normally wins. The impulsiveness and variety of #3 can never get along with the stability and the consistency of #4. On the physical plane they seem to make a good team and this is a strong point in favor of their stability in relationship. Number 3 is passionate, impulsive and demonstrative while #4 is sensitive and sentimental to the needs of love. They enjoy their copulation and this makes up for any differences in other spheres of life.

2-5: The relationship is sexy and adventurous. The #2 is a dedicated housewife and the #5 is an adventurous lover and faithful husband. He will sometimes have to be away from her but will miss her a great deal, and so will she him. When they do get together they will make passionate love together and will enjoy a loving companionship. The #2 must be careful, as her stinging words can be like arrows that will split the heart of her lover. This can make him disheartened, causing sexual inadequacy and loss of sexual satisfaction.

7-9: The two intuitive numbers – imaginative and mysterious #7 combined with the humanitarian and spiritual #9 – represent a supernatural union expressing peace, harmony and happiness for the couple. Both of them are non-materialistic visionaries, mostly away from the physical world, getting too abstract at times. In copulation both of them are imaginative, romantic and demonstrative. Number 9 is passionate and impulsive while #7 is emotional and demanding. They derive the maximum happiness.

8-8: Both of them are equally strong, dynamic, restless and ambitious. They can work tirelessly to achieve power, position and money. They are least concerned with love, harmony or setting a peaceful home. Whenever they work together for a common goal, they reach great heights in accomplishment, which can be a standard example in the world of materialism. And whenever either of them differs from the line of interest there can be chaos and total disaster. In private life both of them are suspicious, jealous and hard in the expression of their affections. They have changing moods and may be seen gentle and romantic one moment and cold and unconcerned the next. Each of them may be spying on one another. They need to reassure each other of their fidelity. However there are rare occasions when both of them are in the right moods for their lovemaking.

Sexual Compatibility Code #8

1-7: The two of them live a harmonious life. Number 1 is a doer, career minded, independent and purposeful, fitting very well with #7, who is intelligent, mysterious and intuitive, supporting each other for further development. On the intimate side the #1 man is passionate and demonstrative and knows how to adjust with the #7 woman. She is neither jealous nor possessive and can use her imagination and intuition to suit her partner. On the other hand if the man is #7 he makes use of his romantic emotionality to combine with the demonstrative nature of the 1 woman. Both of them derive satisfaction on the physical as well as spiritual plane.

2-6: Both of them are evenly balanced, peace loving, passive, romantic and home-loving people, making a very promising couple. Both of them like beauty, harmony and entertaining guests. Number 6 is the caretaker and a natural host/hostess while #2 is the peacemaker. Their home should be well-decorated and full of beautiful things. In private life both of them are gentle, romantic and sentimental, caring more for emotional satisfaction and peace of mind than physical union or the animal passion. The #6 is an evergreen lover – no matter the age – and #2 is romantic. They can spend hours saying nice things to each other. They treat lovemaking very casually and not as a necessity.

3-5: A lot of action and entertainment for the watchers can be found between these two individuals, who are full with energy and restlessness. The #3 man is talented, charming, optimistic, lucky, and likes very much to enjoy the pleasures of life. The #5 woman is very well suited to him since she loves adventure and variety herself. But her love of freedom and taking risks makes her do whatever pleases her and the #3 man cannot contain her. Hence the brakes have to be applied to their speeds, if they want their relationship to remain good. When the man is #5 and the woman is #3 they are more suited to each other. He is adventurous, restless, and needs stimulation every now and then. She is charming and joyous and is the best person to keep him stimulated constantly. Moreover, #5 is changeable and #3 is very lucky so the couple can make the best of every situation. Artistic and creative endeavors of the #3 woman can get a good boost through the constructive criticism of the #5 man. The two of them complement each other nicely, can make good money, and go a long way happily together. In private life there is a lot of excitement. Five is the number of sex, adventure and excitement. Three is the number of excitement, sensuality and pleasure. The two of them indulge in intense lovemaking. But whenever there is a sign of tiredness it shows more of the face of #3 and this can result in #5 wanting to seek pleasure somewhere else.

4-4: A very successful union because both of them are exactly the same – hard working, systematic, brilliant though slow, trustworthy, home loving and very careful in handling money. The negative points can be their non-materialistic interests and melancholic depressions at times. The first thing is taken care of since they are slow but sure and necessary finances grow automatically. The second thing is not for long periods, and gloomy moods are not so serious. From the physical aspect they do not care much for sensual pleasures and are very happy being faithful and considerate to each other. Mutual exchange of love is their policy. They may enjoy lovemaking at times but is not a prerequisite. Neither of them is jealous, suspicious or possessive.

8-9: Both of them are resourceful, charming and good organizers but #8 has the strong desire for power, position and money for self while #9 has the intense desire to serve and help others and work for a common cause. It is here that they differ from each other completely and their views conflict. The intimate side is a difficult one for these two. Number 8 is cold, jealous, suspicious and extremely emotional. Number 9 is charming, passionate and impulsive. If lovemaking is denied to #9 on a few occasions then he/she can be intolerant and furious. Number 9 can adjust with #8 in many things but in matters of sex #8 must be normal and not demanding.

Sexual Compatibility Code #9

1-8: This is a love/hate relationship between two giants, both of whom are strong, tough and fixed in character. They will always try to outdo each other unless they have control over their forceful natures. Both of them are far too proud to say sorry to each other. If #1 decides to use the charm and forgiveness and #8 decides to curb jealousy and mold the emotions cooperatively, the relationship can be a rounding success. Otherwise, it is likely to end in an unmitigated disaster – a divorce or separation is imminent. The #1 man is a passionate lover and if the #8 woman is equally inclined, their enjoyment can be mutual. But if the #8 woman is unprepared, the #1 man cannot force her. On the other hand, if the man is #8 and the woman is #1 she will have to find the right time for copulation. The #8 person should remember that the #1 person can find another partner if love is denied.

2-7: Both of them are imaginative, sensitive, creative, philosophical and spiritual, and likely to make a very peaceful and harmonious life together. Both of them hate arguments and might be equally interested in religious pursuits. The #2 is inclined to follow #7 in most ways, including the interests of #7. Differences can arise when the #2 expresses suspicion and jealousy in the form of accusing #7. The reservation on the one hand and relations with higher ups and people of positions on the other, which #7 has, may create doubts in the mind of #2 and may overreact at times. In such a situation, even a breakup is possible, but the charm and passion of #7 is likely to bring the situation under control. In the department of love, they are likely to have great joys and pleasures. The #7 will take the lead in lovemaking, especially if it is the man, and the #2 will eagerly and willingly respond to the advances of #7.

3-6: The two of them have a very similar nature, complementing each other, and they will pass any test of a good relationship. Both of them have love, charm, creativity and intelligence. There are some problems when the #3 is aggressive or financially wasteful. His #6 wife is cool and well balanced in economic matters and he will have to adjust a bit. Similarly, the #6 woman has to check her habit of taking on too many responsibilities of friends or relatives. The #6 man cannot think of another woman. The two of them make a very good couple.

4-5: 4 is practical and systematic while #5 is imaginative and freedom loving but adjustable. Although the two numbers do not have a common denominator but they are found to complement each other and make a reasonable pair with some adjustments. In private life the #5 person is known to be sexy and demonstrative while the #4 person is loving and considerate but not excited, so the #5 man should try to be gentle with the #4 woman. If the man is #4, he will have to be tactfully controlling the #5 woman and cooperate with her otherwise she finds a way out for her hot-blooded passions.

6-3: In the conjugal relationship the #3 person is passionate, demonstrative and adventurous while the #6 person is also capable of deep love but does not really respond. The #3 man may have to have some extramarital relations at the time, which the 6 woman will ignore since they continue to have a beautiful relationship based on love. If the man is #6, he is able to meet the needs of the #3 woman with his strong physique and romanticism. In general, this Sexual Code presents many hurdles in the couple's sexual life, but with a great deal of understanding and spirituality the couple can experience all the joys of sex in their life.

9-9: This is the relationship of the highest order, full of love, understanding harmony and with a burning desire for the common cause of humanity. Both of them are hard working, intuitive, intelligent, perfectly matched and balanced and knowing each other perhaps for more than a lifetime. They are in complete agreement with each other at all levels of consciousness – physical, mental, emotional, and in intuition. On the intimate side they are the fittest example of relationships. Both of them areloving, passionate and impulsive. The lovemaking brings both spiritual and physical satisfaction full of bliss and fulfillment.

So, there you have it – the explanation of the Sexual Codes. Hopefully you will have a better understanding of your partner's sexual needs and be able to satisfy him or her in a better way.

My book, *The Vedic Sexual Code*, already available explains the Sexual Code in greater detail and will be provide invaluable advice on making your sex and marriage life more enjoyable and fulfilling.

CHAPTER 33

Equation 32 - The Soulmate Code

How to know if Your Partner is Your Soul Mate from a Past Life

Déja vous! You have met this person somewhere in your past before… Are you sure?

Many times people experience the feeling that the person or place they are visiting generates memories that seem to indicate they were there before or knew the person before, even though they have never met in this life or visited this place. This feeling can represent some strange and weird emotions within one and can sometimes make a person feel uncomfortable, too. Because there is belief in reincarnation, this feeling is not uncommon among people but since some other cultures do not accept reincarnation, it presents surprises sometimes within the western person's mind. Many people have consulted with me as to why they are attracted to someone else with a strong passion even though they are married. This is because of something called "Karmic Connection" with that person in a previous life.

Generally everyone and everything we encounter in our life has a "Karmic Connection" with us, but we do not realize these effects unless the connection is very strong, such as in relationships with other people and special places. In this article, I present some of the ways of determining whether you and your partner are soul mates or whether a certain location is where you were before in your past life. If you and your partner have the same Life Codes, then you are soul mates and were together in the past life.

Other factors that indicates previous life experiences can be determined by...

1 When both people have the same birthdays
2 When both people have the same Sun longitude of birth
3 When both people have the same Life Path Codes
4 When both people have the same Moon longitude degree of birth

5   When both people have the same first and middle name
6   When both people have the same birth star constellation degree of birth

Sometimes when sister-in-laws do not agree with each other and they become enemies, it is considered a "Previous Life Connection". When a mother-in-law gets a daughter-in-law that she dislikes, this may also be a Previous Life Connection.

There are repayment Karmic connections such as the right of a lamb that has been killed by a butcher in a previous life will be reborn in this life as a butcher, while the butcher has returned to this life as a lamb. Other connections like these are...

- An employee who has been affected in a drastic way by a boss
- A child that was only allowed to stay a month or less in the world so as to distress a parent who had aborted him before
- A husband who was abusive to his wife in the last life to the point of making her an enemy in the last life, that he dies soon after love connection
- A princess in the last life who is now married back to the prince but he ends up having many affairs because she had rejected him in the last birth.

And many more...

In the following paragraphs, a comparison of the same Life Codes of two people is determined and the results thereof are given.

Life Code #1 Married to Life Code #1

Both persons have the nature of leadership and self-concern. Each one may try to outdo the other in a never-ending game, and it is anybody's guess who will be the winner. The solution can be found in compromise and cooperation by dividing the duties and privileges, etc. This would be easier in a business partnership but not so easy in love and love connection where both have the prestige of their jobs on the one hand and dealing in household chores on the other. The man cannot expect the woman to be waiting for him to serve when he returns home from work. They have to share everything on an equal basis, unless the woman recognizes her femininity and calculates a slight margin for adjustment.

Life Code #2 Married to Life Code #2

Made for each other, identical in most of the ways this combination is a symbol of perfect happiness. The #2 man is not extraordinary in any way but simple, straightforward, secure, one who worries little with no additional involvement, and who longs to come home after work. And the #2 woman just waits for him to return from work and look after him as the ideal man in her life. She is not a career woman and may like to give up her job after love connection to live as a housewife. The two of them do not have to make up any excuse or give any explanation for any shortcomings since they understand each other. They would never like to away from each other even for short periods. Both of them have a touch of spirituality and their interests run almost parallel. At times there can be problems since both of them are shy, lack confidence, suspicious and jealous and quite often under depression.

Life Code #3 Married to Life Code #3

Soul mates, but highly negative. Strong family influence, families disagree on both sides of the love connection partners' family. Childish arguments by the partners usually involving insults to each other's family. Most of the fights will be about family. This love connection is subject to divorce.

Life Code #4 Married to Life Code #4

A very successful union because both of them are exactly the same – hard working, systematic, brilliant though slow, trustworthy, home loving and very careful in handling money. The #4 man will provide security to her, which she needs very much and the #4 woman will take care of him as a perfect housewife. Each of them is a builder and the two of them together will build an excellent home for themselves. The negative points can be their non-materialistic interests and melancholic depressions at times. The first thing is taken care of since they are slow but sure and necessary finances grow automatically. The second thing is not for long periods and gloomy moods are not so serious.

Life Code #5 Married to Life Code #5

Soul mates, but very difficult because of trust issues. Each partner tries to outsmart the other. Each personality thinks that the other won't know that they are doing. This relationship can be highly successful if each partner is honest with each other. The demand for sex is high on both sides. Communication is very important!

Life Code #6 Married to Life Code #6

These two are soul mates, but very childish in their ways. Constant arguments about silly things that are not important will dominate this relationship, if one or both partners are negative. They love children and their first child will always be a boy.

Life Code #7 Married to Life Code #7

Soul mates, they will always think of each other and can never forget their lovemaking moments. Highly egotistical relationship and can separate because of ego, but will constantly come back because of ego, because each partner wants to possess the other. Love connection is highly recommended for this combination.

Life Code #8 Married to Life Code #8

Both of them are equally strong, dynamic, restless and ambitious. They can work tirelessly to achieve power, position and money. They are least concerned with love, harmony or setting a peaceful home. Whenever they work together for a common goal they touch great heights in accomplishment, which can be a standard example in the world of materialism. And whenever either of them differs from the line of interest there can be chaos and total disaster. For success either of them can be selfish and aggressive. When in tune both of them look charming and a dignified couple. Neither of them is unstoppable and unless real care is taken they can actually destroy each other.

Life Code #9 Married to Life Code #9

Soul mates, usually when these two people bring together negative things such as death and sickness happening in the family on both sides. It is highly recommended that a priest be consulted when a love connection between these two is about to take place. They both like to deny their own faults and thus this can become a very negative relationship. Whenever a #9 personality comes into sexual contact with any other of the Life Code, death will occur on one side of the family.

CHAPTER 34

Destruction of the World Trade Center
As Explained by The Vedic Code of Science

If we were to apply the Vedic Code of Science to the World Trade Center incident, we would observe some interesting correlation between what happened on 9/11 and certain events as well as with all the people that were involved. The Vedic Code of Science will attempt to provide a codified view as well as a logical explanation of why the Universe was presenting such an enigma that created such a storm of emotional change throughout the human world.

Let us take a look at the date itself – 9/11, which forms the Life Code 2, which, as indicated in our Table in Chapter 7, is a code of "human relationship."

- The day was the 11th day of September.
- The flight number of the 1st plane that hit was 11.
- The number of people onboard that plane was 92 (9+2=11).
- The Twin Towers had 110 floors (1+1+0=11).
- The Twin Towers standing side by side look like the number 11.
- The number of days from January 1st to 9/11 was 254 (2+5+4=11).
- New York State is the 11th state of the union.
- July 4th as the Life Code of the United States is 11 (7+4=11).

Looking at the names involved in this event will indicate some interesting connections to the number 11.

- New York City - 11 letters
- Afghanistan - 11 letters
- George W. Bush - 11 letters
- Osama bin Laden - 11 letters
- Mohamed Atta - 1st hijacker to hit WTC - 11 letters
- Aran Alshehi - 2nd hijacker to hit WTC - 11 letters
- Rudy Guliani - Mayor of New York City - 11 letters

- Ramzi Yousef - person who unsuccessfully bombed WTC in 1993 - 11 letters
- Colin Powell - US Secretary of State - 11 letters
- USA Pentagon - 11 letters
- Keith Miller - NBC newsman stationed in Islamabad - 11 letters
- Daniel Pearl - reporter killed in Pakistan - 11 letters

After all of the above, one might ask what does #11 have to do with destruction of the WTC? Well, if we were to apply Vedic mathematics to the #11 (1+1) and reduce it to the result of 2, the Vedic Code of love and relationships, we can conclude the following:

Adding the number 2 to the Life Code of the president of the United States, George W. Bush, you get 6 (2+4=6), the Vedic Code that reflects war, destruction and power struggle. Again, if we apply the number 2 from the number 11 to the year 2002, the year following destruction of the WTC, we get the number 6 (2+2+0+0+2=6), the Code of war, destruction and power struggle (USA v UN on Iraq War). The US did go to war with Iraq.

We all know that the Book of Revelations in the Bible considers the number 666 an evil number. Please note that when we add the number 666 in Vedic mathematics (6+6+6), the result is 18, which is then further reduced to 9, the Code of death and termination. Well, if we were to take all the 11 numbers from the previous results and add each 11 to the year 2002, the result would be 66666666...for all the names and codes involve on the date of 9/11.

Applying the Code of death and termination – 9 – to the World Trade Center events, we find some interesting connections between this code and the people and dates involved.

If we take the Code of change (#5) and add it to the Life Code of President Bush (#4), the result is Life Code 9; again death, destruction and power struggle related to the United States.

It was exactly 9 years before – in 1993 – when the first attempt was made to destroy the World Trade Center. If we take the Life Code of the USA (2) and add it to the year 1993 (4), we get 6, which is the Code of struggle and war.

If we were to add the Code of War (6) to the year 2001 (3), the result is Life Code 9, the code of death and destruction (6+1001=9).

According to Vedic Science, the Eastern year for harvest begins every September of the Western year. According to Eastern timing, 2002 would be considered the year ruling at the time of the 9/11 events. If we were to take Western year 2001 and add it to the Eastern year of 2002 and then add it to the Event Code of 11, the result would be Life Code 9, the code of death and destruction.

If we take the Code of Travel (5) and add it to the year 2002, the result would be 9 (5+2002), the Code of death and destruction. We all know that the travel industry almost came to a halt and the airline and ground transportation industries for travelers suffered great losses. Traveling became very difficult and uncomfortable for a great many people in the United States and abroad. Many airlines filed bankruptcy in the courts and many people lost their money in the industry.

The New Millennium

There was a clear misconception by the world about the actual time when the new millennium started. The new millennium actually began on January 1, 2001; however, the whole world was led to believe that it started in January 2000 by the computer companies that installed the fear of Y2K disasters in the minds of people. Because of this, people did not realize that the world actually experienced a great renewal and awakening in the 9th month of the new millennium, really 2001.

A look at the years from 1989 (9) to the year 2001 (3) reveals an astounding continuity in the events that proceeded 9/11/2001. Please bear in mind that if we were to take all the years from 600 BC to 1989, only the years 1899 and 1989 would add up to 27 or triple 9 (9+9+9). The world experienced significant changes in these years. Let us take a serious look at the years previous to the new millennium...the eventful 90s.

1989 - Communism took a fall and most of the countries in the world became democratic.
1990 - Violence increased considerably among the Middle Eastern

countries starting with the letter "I" – Iran, Iraq, and Israel. Saddam Hussein began to be troublesome to the USA.

1991 - The Gulf War between the US and Iraq took place, but was not effective enough to stop the power of Saddam Hussein. The war lasted 45 days, the time it takes for the planet Mars to traverse 30 degrees of the zodiac.

1992 - Osama bin Laden appeared as the Turban Terrorist, and the strongest hurricane ever to hit the US – Hurricane Andrew – caused enormous damage to the state of Florida.

1993 - Attempts to bomb and destroy the World Trade Center failed and the terrorist, Ramzi Yousef, swore that his organization would be back to destroy it, as he was being taken to prison.

1994 - The most renowned murder trial of the decade began – the O. J. Simpson case. The Eiffel Tower in Paris, France was the target of terrorists.

1995 - Over 200 US soldiers were killed in a US training center bombed by terrorists.

1996 - The apartment complex for Americans in Teheran, Iran was bombed by terrorists; many were killed.

1997 - Many tourists, including Americans, were killed in a bombing incident in Egypt, again by terrorists.

1998 - The US Embassy in Africa was destroyed by a terrorist bombing.

1999 - The US sailor ship was destroyed at sea by terrorism. The largest sex scandal trial ever, that of US President Bill Clinton, began.

2000 - The election scandal of the US – the people had a choice – election or selection of the US president. George Bush won by Supreme Court decision, the first time in the history of the USA.

2001 - The destruction of the World Trade Center occurred exactly 9 years after the first attempt in 1993. The world experienced a new awakening towards the religion of Islam.

2002 - Another member of the Bush family – George W. – launched a pre-emptive war against Saddam Hussein of Iraq, a promise kept by the Elder Bush that he would return to get Saddam. The planet Mars comes closest to the Earth in centuries.

Nostradamus predicted centuries before the rise of the Turban Warrior from the East that we saw played out here in history. The vents of the "destructive 90s" led eventually to the rude awakening of human existence after the destruction of the World Trade Center in 2001.

As you can see, the Vedic Code of Science clearly indicates that death and destruction were events that Nostradamus predicted, that in the 9th month of the new millennium, the "New City" would face destruction as it was struck by two "birds from above. The 90s were a period pre-empting this reawakening of the human race. Because of all the world events that took place in the previous century, which are considered negative, the Earth and the Universe has created a reaction that will help bring about a great change in human thinking and awareness. All religions will be questioned about their validity in being genuine in the progress of human thought. People will question whether astrology, spirituality and other forms of worship are really helping them in their lives. People will seek other forms of explanations for life and the future of the world. People will seek more technical details on how to be safer in the world and enjoy their family lives in a more secure way.

Only in times of distress or war that mankind seeks other means or methods of making or preserving peace on Earth. Only in times of suffering will people seek to come closer to God. To illustrate my point, let us look at the following story, called "Light vs. Darkness".

At one time in the Universe, there was an argument between LIGHT and DARKNESS. LIGHT insisted that she was more important to humans because she provided enlightenment, comfort, wealth, and beauty to them. DARKNESS disagreed, saying he was more important to humans because whenever he provided humans with arrogance, discomfort, poverty, and suffering, they would seek Godly messages and the advice of holy people. Since both LIGHT and DARKNES could not come to an agreement as to which one was more important, they sought the advice of the CREATOR. Feeling he would appear biased if he made a choice, the CREATOR decided to send them to the UNIVERSE. On their arrival there, the UNIVERSE welcomed both LIGHT and DARKNES and smiled, saying, "You are both important, LIGHT and DARKNESS.

However, LIGHT, you are important only when you are coming into a person's life...and DARKNESS, you are very important only when you are leaving a person's life."

As you can see from the story above, humans, the Universe, and the Earth must be so balanced that light and darkness cannot affect them unevenly. People need to learn to enjoy the world in equilibrium before they can live happily.

CHAPTER 35

Special Note on the Power of
Life Code #6 – The Vedic Science Code of Kali

Small droplets of water condensing into storm clouds and falling earthward through cold layers of the atmosphere cannot "think." Yet one of these droplets, when it freezes, forms a flat hexagonal crystal. Countless billions of them comprise tiny snowflakes, each with six sides or arms – and each one different than all the others. No two ever alike, infinite variation and endless beauty. How does this happen? Why don't they sometimes have eight or ten sides or four?

A snowflake is a crystal of frozen water; a diamond is a crystal of "frozen" carbon. One is formed in the atmosphere, the other within the mantle of the Earth. One has six sides, the other 12. Each seems to conform to the geomagnetic field and/or celestial magnetic field. They cannot "think." They have no instinct, let alone reason; therefore, exogenous forces must act upon them.

Distant stars, great nations and tiny snowflakes all are inextricably intertwined. Weather conditions are strongly responsive to the crystallizing 60-degree angle between planets. This 60-degree (hexagon) was considered by all ancient civilizations to be "sacred." Two perfect triangles of 120 degrees when placed together form the symbol of Judaism, the Star of David. Each point of this star is 60 degrees to the next.

Bees all over the world build hexagonal honeycombs. It is "unthinkable" that bees, of their own intelligence, consciously agree to this standard. Only recently have engineers discovered that the hexagon is the strongest, most economical storage bin imaginable. Yet bees have always "known" this, but how? By instinct? If so, exactly what is this instinct? How does it differ from free choice?

How do bees all over the world (ever since bees were "invented") build six-sided storage bins for their honey? They've always done it and probably will continue doing so for as long as there are bees.

In the Vedic Code of Science, 6 is considered a code that represents power, destruction, frustration and great emotional upheaval in relationships between all things. The Life Code of 6 represents the influences of war, conflicts between people, war between countries, separation of couples and such things as mortgages, debts, credit cards and loans. You'll find that the police or security forces of a country are represented by the Life Code #6. An analysis of the Life Codes of all the police or military members would reveal a predominant number of them that add up to the Life Code of 6.

In the Vedic Code of Science, the God of negative time and destruction of evil is known as Kali, the sixth form of the female goddesses. She is known as the caretaker of the rules of the Universe. When the rules are broken and evil thoughts, acts or intentions threaten the Universe, Kali is the one who corrects the person or destroys the evil permanently.

People with Life Codes that add up to the Life Code 6 usually experience a lot of traffic tickets in their life, court problems and accidents, if they live a negative lifestyle. If they live a positive lifestyle, they will experience power, luxury, great reputation in their career, family inheritance and popularity. Usually getting a government position helps to uplift the life of Kali people in a positive manner.

The year 1961 is made up of the numbers 6 and 9. When turned upside down, the numbers remain the same.

The number 9 has remarkable inversion properties. When reversed, it becomes a 6. When added to 6 it becomes 15, which if you add 1+5, you get 6. If we take the number 133335 and add up the digits, the result is 9. If we take the reverse of this number 533331 and add them to the original number, the result is 666,666, a double form of evil.

The 6th planet from the Sun is Saturn. The number 6 also rules Mars. Both of these planets are considered negative planets in astrological science.

The Life Code of 6 rules such things as violence, assassinations, violent deaths and separations. Interestingly, the highest office with the most power is the office of American president. The first president, George Washington, had a Life Code of 6 (February 22). President Harrison, whose Life Code was 2 (February 9), when added to April 4, 1841, you get the Day Code of 6, when he died in office.

President Abraham Lincoln, whose Life Code was 5 (February 12), was assassinated and died in office. The day he died, Life Code 1 (April 15), when added to his Life Code, gives the Life Code of 6, which indicates violent death. President William McKinley, who had a Life Code of 3 (January 29), when added to the day he was shot in office (September 6), gives the Death Code of 9. McKinley died 8 days later on September 14, 1901.

President Warren Harding, whose Life Code was 4 (November 2), when added to the Day Code (August 2) gives the Life Code of 6. He died in office after a heart attack. The Life Code of 6 (November 22) was also ruling at the time that President Kennedy was shot.

The first President Bush, elected in 1989, has a Life Code of 9 (June 12). He was the first US president to take America into war after Viet Nam. If you remember also that President Lyndon Johnson, the 36th (Life Code 9) US president, whose Life Code was 8 (August 27), elected in a year (1963), which when added to his Life Code results in 9 (code of struggle). He was the president that started the Viet Nam War.

Bill Clinton, whose Life Code is 9, was troubled by terrorist bombings throughout his term in office. He was also the first president to be impeached by the House of Representatives.

The present President, George W. Bush, whose Life Code is 4 (July 6), when added to the birthday of America (July 4) comes out to the Life Code of 6, the code of war.   He restarted his father's legacy of war in Iraq. Please note his inaugural Day Code 2 (January 20), when added to his Life Code, results in the Life Code 6. Hence, as long as he is president of the United States, the country will be at war.

It will take a strong personality like Hillary Clinton to take us out of war. Please note that the planet Mars, which started its journey toward Earth when George W. Bush took office, is going to recede after the 2006 elections, hence the return of the troops.

APPENDIX 1

The Other Life Codes

YOUR WORLD CODE
THE COUNTRY CODE
THE STREET CODE
THE TELEPHONE CODE
THE BUSINESS PARTNERSHIP CODE
THE ENEMY CODE
THE SEQUENCE CODE
THE DIET CODE
THE LONGEVITY CODE
THE SATURN EFFECT CODE
THE HATE CODE
THE STAGES OF LIFE CODE
THE DEATH CODE
THE INSANITY CODE
THE ORAL SEX CODE
THE ANCESTRAL CODE
THE LAST CHILD CODE
THE HOUR CODE
THE LIFE CODE OF BRAMHA
THE LIFE CODE OF DURGA
THE LIFE CODE OF VISHNU
THE LIFE CODE OF RUDRA
THE LIFE CODE OF NARAYAN
THE LIFE CODE OF KALI
THE LIFE CODE OF SHIVA
THE LIFE CODE OF LAXMI
THE LIFE CODE OF INDRA
THE LIFE CODE OF YAMA
THE UNIVERSAL CODE
THE YEARLY CODES

APPENDIX 2

Famous People & Their Life Codes

"Some are born great, some achieve greatness, and some have greatness thrust upon them." – William Shakespeare

You may use the information in this chapter to test the Science of Vedic Codes. Using the codes provided, you can observe the characteristics and personality of famous people and see if they match your Life Code analysis.

Name	Birthdate	Life Code#
Lord Russell	August 12	1
Empress Eugene	May 5, 2006	1
Mesmer	May 23	1
Karl Marx	May 5	1
Fahrenheit	May 14	1
Oliver Cromwell	April 24	1
Sir Isaac Newton	December 25	1
Bloody Queen Mary	February 17	1
Theodore Roosevelt	October 27	1
General Gordon	January 28	2
Annie Besant	October 1	2
Captain Cook	October 28	2
Nathaniel Hawthorne	July 4	2
Duke of Windsor	June 23	2
Duke of Marlborough	May 24	2
Mary, Queen of Scots	December 8	2
Queen Victoria	May 24	2
William Wordsworth	April 7	2
Rousseau	April 16	2
King Edward VII	November 9	2

William Garfield	November 19	3
Mahatma Gandhi	October 2	3
Lal Bahadur Shastri	October 2	3
Swedenborg	January 29	3
Thomas Hood	May 23	3
Queen Josephine	June 23	3
Robert Browning	May 7	3
Kepler	December 27	3
Woodrow Wilson	December 28	4
Queen Alexandra	December 1	4
Thomas Edison	February 11	4
Marie Antoinette	November 2	4
Thomas Chatterton	November 20	4
Ramsay MacDonald	October 12	4
Louis XVI	August 23	4
Cecil Rhodes	July 6	4
Ralph Waldo Emerson	June 25	4
Leopold II of Belgium	April 9	4
Ulysses S. Grant	April 27	4
Louis Kossuth	April 27	4
James Monroe	April 28	5
Otto von Bismarck	April 1	5
Gladstone	December 29	5
Abraham Lincoln	February 12	5
Voltaire	November 21	5
Dean Swift	November 30	5
Cardinal Newman	February 21	5
Mark Twain	November 30	5
Winston Churchill	November 30	5
Faraday	October 22	5
Lord Byron	January 22	5
Schubert	January 31	5

Sir Isaac Pitman	January 4	5
Sir Francis Bacon	January 22	5
Cardinal Richelieu	September 5	5
Napoleon I	August 15	5
Lord Alfred Tennyson	August 6	5
Lord Balfour	July 25	5
John Wesley	June 17	5
Bruce Jenner	June 17	5
Prince Albert/Monaco	August 26	5
Nicholas II of Russia	May 18	5
Sir James Barrie	May 9	5
Duke of Wellington	May 1	6
Napoleon III	April 20	6
George Pullman	March 3	6
Rudyard Kipling	December 30	6
Lord Baden Powell	February 22	6
George Elliot	November 22	6
George Washington	February 22	6
Subhas Bose	January 23	6
John D. Rockefeller	July 8	6
La Fontaine	July 8	6
George Bernard Shaw	July 26	6
George Stephenson	June 9	6
Brigham Young	June 1	7
Thomas Carlyle	December 4	7
Hinrieh Heine	December 13	7
Jawaharlal Nehru	November 14	7
Samuel Pepys	February 23	7
Tallyrand	February 14	7
Joan of Arc	January 6	7
Frederick the Great	January 24	7
George Westinghouse	October 6	7

Bonar Law	September 16	7
Louis XIV	September 16	7
Queen Elizabeth	September 7	7
Alexander the Great	July 1	8
Alexandre Dumas	July 28	8
Orville Wright	August 19	8
Thomas Hardy	June 2	8
Immanuel Kant	April 22	8
Sir Henry Irving	February 6	8
John Knox	November 24	8
Oscar Wilde	October 16	8
Richard I Lion-Hearted	September 8	8
Herbert Hoover	August 10	9
King George V	June 3	9
Sir Arthur Conan Doyle	May 22	9
Thomas Huxley	May 4	9
William Shakespeare	April 23	9
Elizabeth Browning	March 6	9
Michelangelo	March 6	9
Sir Walter Scott	December 6	9
Max Muller	December 6	9
King George	December 24	9
Warren Hastings	December 6	9
Andrew Carnegie	November 25	9
Wilkie Collins	January 8	9
David Lloyd George	January 17	9

APPENDIX 3

Birthdates & Life Codes of
Famous People & Major Events

Famous Name	Date	Life Code
Muhammed Ali	01/18/1942	1
Warren Beatty	03/30/1937	6
Marlon Brando	04/03/1924	7
Tom Brokaw	02/06/1940	8
Charles Bronson	11/03/1922	5
Carol Burnett	04/26/1933	3
Johnny Carson	10/23/1925	6
Jimmy Carter	10/14/1924	6
Fidel Castro	08/13/1946	3
Prince Charles	11/14/1948	7
Cher	05/20/1946	7
Dick Clark	03/30/1945	6
Bill Clinton	08/19/1946	9
Hillary Clinton	10/16/1947	9
Bill Cosby	07/12/1937	1
Ted Danson	12/29/1947	5
Robert DeNiro	08/17/1943	7
Phil Donahue	12/21/1935	6
Michael Douglas	09/25/1944	7
Clint Eastwood	05/31/1930	9
Jane Fonda	12/21/1937	6
Gerald Ford	07/14/1913	3
Harrison Ford	07/04/1942	2
Al Gore	03/31/1948	7
Tipper Gore	08/19/1948	9

Goldie Hawn	11/21/1945	5
Hugh Hefner	04/09/1926	4
DustinHoffman	08/08/1937	7
Bob Hope	05/29/1903	7
Michael Jackson	8/28/1958	9
Jesse Jackson	10/08/1941	9
Ann Jillian	01/29/1950	3
Pope John Paul II	05/18/1920	5
Jerry Lewis	05/16/1926	3
Andrea Macko	10/28/1966	2
Kamini Maragh	04/12/1968	7
Ramesh Maragh	01/30/1964	4
Dean Martin	06/17/1917	5
Paul McCartney	06/18/1942	6
Paul Newman	01/26/1925	9
Jack Nicholson	04/22/1937	8
Richard Nixon	01/08/1913	1
Al Pacino	04/25/1940	2
Dolly Parton	01/19/1946	2
Elvis Presley	01/08/1935	9
Richard Pryor	12/01/1940	4
Nancy Reagan	07/06/1923	4
Ronald Reagan	02/06/1911	8
Robert Redford	08/18/1937	8
Burt Reynolds	02/11/1936	4
Diana Ross	03/26/1944	2
Brooke Shields	05/31/1965	9
Frank Sinatra	12/12/1917	6
Steven Spielberg	12/18/1947	3
Bruce Springsteen	09/23/1949	5
Sly Stallone	07/06/1946	4
James Stewart	05/20/1908	7

Meryl Streep	06/22/1949	1
Barbra Streisand	04/24/1942	1
Elizabeth Taylor	02/27/1932	2
John Travolta	02/18/1954	2
Barbara Walters	09/25/1931	7
Stevie Wonder	05/13/1950	9
Tammy Wynette	05/05/1942	1
Jeffrey Dahmer	05/21/1966	8
Jerry Rubin	07/14/1938	3
Empress Nagako	03/06/1905	9
Alex Trebek's daughter	08/16/1993	6
Stewart Granger	05/06/1913	2
Alan Dershowitz	09/01/1938	1
Christie Brinkley's son	06/02/1995	8
Elizabeth Montgomery	04/15/1933	1
Angier Biddle Duke	11/20/1915	4
Erich Leinsdorf	02/04/1912	6
Nancy Kerrigan	10/13/1970	5
Jorge Luis Borges	08/24/1899	5
Frederico Fellini	01/20/1920	3
Cesar Romero	02/15/1907	8
Norman Vincent Peale	05/31/1898	9
Robert Cecil Williams	01/10/1909	2
Bill Bixby	01/22/1934	5
David Koresh	09/15/1959	6
Joey Buttafucco	03/11/1956	5
Darzen Petrovic	10/22/1964	5
Kathie Lee Gifford	08/16/1953	6
Vita Sackville-West	03/09/1892	3
Rush Limbaugh	01/12/1951	4
Mikhail Gorbachev	03/02/1931	5
Prince Takahito Mikasa	12/02/1915	5

Shu Kawashima	07/26/1973	6
Misugu Akimoto	06/01/1955	7
Takuma Miyamoto	01/09/1993	1
Danny DeVito	11/17/1944	1
Magic Johnson	06/04/1992	1
Brennan Karem	06/26/1992	5
Tiffany Trump	10/13/1993	5
Montel Williams II	09/17/1993	8
Vesna Vulovic	08/06/1949	5
Slobodan Milosevic	08/20/1940	1
Mickey Mouse	11/18/1928	2
Michael Caine	03/14/1933	8
Frank Sinatra	12/12/1915	6
Dodi al Fayed	04/15/1955	1
Gianni Versace	12/02/1946	5
Drew Carey	05/23/1958	1
Luis Donaldo Colosio	02/10/1950	3
Arsenio Hall	02/12/1956	5
Augustine Ann Brooks	05/03/1994	8

Event	Date	Life Code
Birth on the highway	07/14/1938	3
Dangerous fire	08/08/1994	7
Kitchen fire	08/07/1994	6
House fire	12/21/1994	6
House fire	12/20/1994	5
House fire	12/17/1994	5
Cruise ship inferno	11/30/1994	5
Explosion/NY subway	12/21/1994	6
Baby born on freeway	02/03/1995	5
Dead back to life	10/29/1993	3

Norway tankers collide	02/05/1995	7
Chinese rocket blows	01/26/195	9
Car bomb kills dozens	01/30/1995	4
Truck kills 7 at school	08/13/1993	3
Ca traffic pile-up	11/29/1991	4
Chris Reeves accident	05/27/1995	5
Hidden gun law/TX	05/26/1995	4
Earthquake in Russia	05/28/1995	6
Deadly subway crash	06/05/1995	2
Car bomb in Peru	05/24/1994	2
Dispatcher aids birth	01/08/1994	9
LA earthquake	01/17/1994	9
Killer tornado, OK	04/24/1993	1
Argentina tornado	05/06/1992	2
Argentina tornado	11/25/1985	9
Volcano eruption	10/18/1992	1
Monica Seles stabbing	04/30/1993	7
Royal wedding, Japan	06/09/1993	6
Restore hope	12/09/1992	3
Clinton's mother dies	11/19/1992	3
Windsor Castle fire	11/20/1992	4
Reba McEntire crash	11/06/1992	8
Oil tanker crash, Spain	12/03/1992	6
Baby left in -0°	02/02/1993	4
Birth in custody	01/18/1993	1
Baby born on subway	01/11/1993	3
Abandoned baby	01/06/1993	7
Israel-Palestine Accord	09/13/1993	4
Chicago storm	07/02/1992	9
CA Angels bus crash	05/21/1992	8
Tragic car crash	06/02/1992	8
Addict kills parents	03/26/1970	2

Irish cease fire	08/31/1994	3
USAir crash	09/08/1994	8
Penn Station blaze	09/11/1994	2
Oklahoma City blast	04/19/1999	5
Fatal tornado	03/27/1956	3
Killer bee attack	11/03/1994	5